# The Ethics of Belief
# An Essay on The Victorian
# Religious Conscience

AAR STUDIES IN RELIGION
Number Nine

# The Ethics of Belief
# An Essay on The Victorian
# Religious Conscience

by
JAMES C. LIVINGSTON
The College of William and Mary in Virginia

Tallahassee, Florida
American Academy of Religion
1974

Distributed by
SCHOLARS PRESS
University of Montana
Missoula, Montana 59801


Copyright © 1974
American Academy of Religion


**Library of Congress Cataloging in Publication Data**

Livingston, James C.          1930-
    The ethics of belief.

    (AAR studies in religion : no. 9)
    Includes bibliographical references.
    1. Great Britian—Religion—19th century. 2. Ethics
—History—Great Britian. I. Title. II. Series:
American Academy of Religion. AAR studies in religion;
no. 9.
BR759.L55          170'.942          74-18616
ISBN 0-88420-121-X

COMPOSED IN TIMES ROMAN TYPE AT THE U. of M. PRINTING DEPARTMENT
PRINTED IN THE UNITED STATES OF AMERICA
PRINTING DEPARTMENT, UNIVERSITY OF MONTANA,
MISSOULA, MONTANA 59801

# Preface

A few words of acknowledgment and appreciation are especially in order. My serious interest in late Victorian religious thought began a few years ago, about the time that Van Harvey was publishing some of his work on the ethics of belief in the context of contemporary theology. I found Harvey's work very congenial, particularly because I thought theology had gotten lost in the fog of the new hermeneutics. I soon discovered that the Victorians were absorbed with the question of the morality of religious knowledge and I recognized in these figures a host of kindred spirits.

I began this study with the debates of the Metaphysical Society between 1869 and 1880 and this led me both backward to the 1840's and forward into the second decade of this century. The figure who remains a constant presence in the discussion through the mid-Victorian era is John Henry Newman. While I bring Newman into my account at several points, an essay such as this can't do full justice to the important role he played in this debate throughout the period.

This study constitutes one aspect of a larger exploration of late Victorian religious thought, undertaken through the assistance of the American Council of Learned Societies, of which I served as a Fellow during 1972-73.

Much of the research and writing of this essay was done in the University Library, Cambridge, of which I have the fondest memories. I owe a considerable debt of gratitude to the University Library staff for their many services and kindnesses.

The Editor of this series, Stephen Crites, gave me wise counsel and his careful reading of the text spared the reader several ambiguities and infelicities of style which I had not detected.

The College of William and Mary
July, 1974

"Faith must give the last word; but the last word is not the whole utterance of the truth: the whole truth is that assurance and doubt must alternate in the moral world in which we at present live."

Henry Sidgwick

# I

The Victorian era was an age of faith. It was also a time when that faith underwent a series of severe crises. The great unsettlement felt by sensitive Englishmen in the late 19th century is traceable to what Lord Acton has called the Victorian's "intense need of believing and the difficulty of belief." This Victorian distraction is understandable when it is clear the extent to which the Victorian conscience was torn between two moral commitments: viz., to a scrupulous intellectual honesty and the demand for a forthright assent to the creeds and formularies of the Church of England. The Victorian "clerisy" were gripped by a passion for sincerity such as the world has seldom seen. Whether this quest of the "honest soul" is admirable or morbid in the extreme has long been a matter of debate. But it was, perhaps, *the* mark of the Victorian character. John Henry Newman's brother Francis, an unbeliever still in the grip of an Evangelical conscience, wrote that "The question must always be, not whether the argument be positive or negative, but whether it is *true*."[1] T. H. Huxley never tired of preaching the conviction that "the most sacred act of a man's life is to say and to feel, 'I believe such and such to be true'."[2] "My only desire," wrote George Eliot, "is to know the truth, my only fear to cling to error."[3] And it was the sage Carlyle who gave the Victorians their motto: "Truth, though the heavens crush me for following it."

It was in this moral climate that the clergy and educated laity had week in, week out to give both mental and verbal assent to the creeds and doctrines of the church—at a time of advancing religious criticism and unsettlement. Out of this complex of factors there emerged an extended, often acrimonious and divisive series of controversies over the morality of belief.

Much of the debate focused on the ethics of conformity and subscription to the creeds and formularies of the church. Laymen in the Church of England were not required to adhere to any particular doctrine, although it was expected that they could in good conscience recite the words of the liturgy. But those who would take holy orders or those who would matriculate as students or hold fellowships and teaching appointments in the colleges in Oxford or Cambridge faced stricter requirements. Prior to the mid 1850's young men entering the colleges were solemnly obliged to subscribe to the Thirty-nine Articles of Religion. It was not until 1871, when the Gladstone government passed the universities tests act, that all degrees and appointments, excepting those requiring holy orders, were exempted from subscription to the Articles. Before the clerical subscription act of 1865 men taking orders were required to acknowledge "all and every article to be agreeable to the word of God." After 1865 assent to the Articles became general rather than particular. This freed the consciences of some but it became, as we shall see, cause of renewed controversy and an added burden to many sensitive minds who felt that the binding force of subscription was relaxed at the sacrifice of scrupulous veracity. The movement for revision or relaxation began, however, much earlier.

Three years after Queen Victoria's accession to the throne the issue of liberalizing subscription was brought before the House of Lords. A petition presented by Archbishop Whately asked that the Articles be made consonant with the beliefs of the clergy. Probably not much would have come of the matter had it not been for a speech by Bishop Stanley of Norwich. He spoke of the "elasticity" of the Church of England, of the fact that not all clergy agreed with every part of their subscription, and that such latitude was sound. He pointed out that the Church's creed was Calvinistic, while its liturgy was Arminian. The speech offended most everyone. Conscientious clergymen didn't like to be told that the church was lax or indifferent concerning what it believed, and the Tractarian party was horrified to hear a bishop declare the Church's Articles Calvinistic. The Tractarians replied with John Henry Newman's Tract XC, which sought to defend a Catholic interpretation of the Articles.

It was this event, more than any other, that focused the attention of the English "clerisy" on the issue of religious belief and created a climate of suspicion and doubt. It brought down on Newman a flood of charges of disingenuousness in the use of reserve and equivocation in his apology for the Catholic faith. Tract XC appeared to many to evade the plain meaning of the Thirty-nine Articles. Newman admitted as much. "I have asserted," he wrote, "a great principle, and I ought to suffer for it, that the Articles are to be interpreted, not according to the meaning of the writers, but, so far as the wording will admit, according to the sense of the Catholic Church."

That Newman appeared to evade the clear meaning of the Articles was especially true of his treatment of such matters as the Articles' condemnation of the doctrine of purgatory and the sacrifice of masses. Newman's casuistry discovered that Article XXII condemning the "Romish" doctrine of purgatory was not directed at the Roman Catholic doctrine, since that doctrine was not formulated at the Council of Trent until after Article XXII was drafted. Such interpretive sleight-of-hand was repulsive to many. Of course, the real fear was that if such liberties were allowed there would be no fence against Roman Catholic teaching in the Church of England. Nevertheless, Newman's apparent sophistry dismayed and alarmed friend and foe alike.

Several bishops condemned Tract XC and Bishop Bagot of Oxford was called upon to have it suppressed. Newman resisted such a move and threatened to resign. It was finally agreed that publication of the Tracts would cease at the bishop's insistence, but that Tract XC would not be censured. Bishop Bagot respected the Tractarians' piety and dutifulness and was loath to condemn them. Yet it is obvious that the subtlety and evasion of Tract XC disturbed the bishop, as it did so many others. Having agreed not to censure, he could not, in a charge in St. Mary's Church, Oxford, in 1842, refrain from declaring his objection to "a system of interpretation that is so subtle, that by it the Articles may be made to mean anything or nothing."[4] Those words were to become a common refrain in the years ahead.

The importance of Newman as catalyst of this new solicitude over sincerity of belief cannot be exaggerated. The special role that he played in the Victorian debate over the ethics of belief is reflected not only in the Tract XC affair but also in the controversy with Charles Kingsley which launched Newman on the writing of the *Apologia*, and in the vigorous debates over *A Grammar of Assent* during the early 1870's.

The story of how the *Apologia* came to be written is well known to those familiar with Newman's life, but it can be briefly recapitulated here. Late in 1863 there appeared in *Macmillan's Magazine* a review by Charles Kingsley of J. A. Froude's *History of England*, Volumes VII and VIII. Kingsley took the occasion to attack the Roman Church for the deceit and laxity that he found rife in Europe. "Truth for its own sake," wrote Kingsley "had never been a virtue with the Roman clergy. Father Newman informs us that it need not and, on the whole, ought not be."[5] Newman protested and there followed an exchange of letters between the two men. Kingsley offered a public apology but included in it the following: "No man knows the use of words better than Dr. Newman; no man, therefore, has a better right to define what he does, or does not mean by them. It only remains, therefore, for me to express my hearty regret at having so seriously mistaken him; and my hearty pleasure at finding him on the side of Truth . . ."[6] The apology appeared feigned, for Kingsley left the clear impression of duplicity on Newman's part. Newman countered by publishing, to Kingsley's horror, the entire correspondence between them. Kingsley replied in turn with a pamphlet, "What, Then, Does Mr. Newman Mean?" He charged that Newman's Anglican sermons were dishonest since they, in fact, preached Roman doctrine. It was this charge that forced Newman to defend his Anglican career and that produced the *Apologia*.[7]

It is generally conceded that Kingsley's "rash accusations" against Newman's *personal* honesty were rebutted in the exchange between the two men and in Newman's *Apologia*. Nevertheless, eminent men remained convinced of Newman's personal dishonesty. Benjamin Jowett pronounced that "in speculation (Newman) was habitually untruthful and not much better in practice." Huxley held Newman to be "the slipperiest sophist I have ever met with," and thought Kingsley "was entirely right about him."[8] Newman's fellow Roman Catholic, the historian Lord Acton, claimed that it was Newman's practice "not to say the truth, if it injures religious interest."[9] Whether these are fair judgments of Newman's personal honesty remains moot. Nevertheless, Kingsley's accusation that Newman's writings *encouraged* lack of candor and disingenuousness in religious teaching found widespread support with critics such as Leslie and Fitzjames Stephen, Huxley, Jowett, Mark Pattison, Acton, and Frederick Meyrick. These criticisms were not, nor can they be, simply swept aside.[10]

It was in this climate, rife with charges of credulity and dishonesty, that the controversy over *Essays and Reviews* (1860) arose, of far-reaching significance for English religion. On one level, *Essays and Reviews* marked another significant chapter in the long contest between the established tradition and authority of the church and the claims of critical scholarship. But, as in the case of Newman in a different context, the substantive issues, involving questions of the legitimacy of the methods and findings of literary-historical criticism, were often ignored while attention was focused on the moral honesty of the essayists, teaching the things they did as clergymen of the Church of England.

The seven essayists were roundly condemned and the book was firmly denounced by the bishops in Convocation. The essayists were labeled the *Septem Contra Christum*. What were condemned by Pusey and others as blasphemous errors are today admitted by the widest criticism as commonplace. But more significantly, not only the essayists' theories but their moral integrity was recklessly and bitterly impugned. "The question before us," wrote one Oxonian, "concerns not the truth of their new doctrines but the honesty of the writers . . . it is a question of public morality and what intimately touches the national conscience," for "the honest instincts of the nation revolt at connivance with such dishonesty."[11] Many felt that it was the bishops who were answerable for winking at such "affected reverence," but it was not long before Bishop Wilberforce, as on other occasions quick to the challenge, threw down the gauntlet. Wilberforce's charge against the seven was widely shared; it also points up the underlying problem and tragic confusion at the center of this and future controversies over the ethics of clerical subscription.

At the conclusion of an extended criticism of *Essays and Reviews*, Wilberforce wrote that he felt bound to express his conviction "that holding their views, (the essayists) cannot, consistently with moral honesty, maintain their posts as clergymen of the Established Church."[12] Wilberforce believed that men such as Frederick Temple, Jowett, and Rowland Williams countenanced doubt and hence unbelief. "Doubt itself is not sinful" but "it is the allowance and the encouragement of doubting which is sinful."[13] And yet throughout the controversy Wilberforce could be heard iterating that "there is amongst us not permitted only, but encouraged, the largest allowance of free thought compatible with teaching honestly."[14] But what does "teaching honestly" entail? For Wilberforce honest teaching required teaching the church's doctrines "not as an inquiring philosophy, but as a revealed truth."[15] While disparaging an unthinking clergy, the Bishop of Oxford, nevertheless, charged that a clergyman "may think as he will, but he must teach both what he thinks and what he is pledged to teach." If he cannot harmonize the two then "he must lay down his teacher's office."[16]

At first glance this may appear a straightforward request for candid action, but it fails to meet the crucial issue. In 1860 an English cleric was bound to "an unfeigned assent and consent to all and everything" within the Prayer Book, and "to all and everyone of the Articles"—but with one formidable qualification , viz., that those doctrines and formularies are "proved by the most certain warrants of Scripture." The Church of England grounds its beliefs in the warrant of Scripture, but how, one must ask, does one establish the true meaning and intent of Scripture except by allowing the scholar to pursue his literary and historical studies unfettered by preconceived notions?

In the heat of battle over *Essays and Reviews*, Wilberforce published two sermons on the subject of religious doubt, counseling that a man ought to "fling it from him as if it were a loaded shell shot into the fortress of his soul." Once again the Bishop failed to make plain the difference between inquiry and what he called "sinful doubt." The sermons met with a chorus of replies from, among others, Goldwyn Smith, John Malcolm Ludlow and F. D. Maurice. "A religion," wrote Smith, "which should adopt your Lordship's advocacy, and say with you 'fling away doubt' . . . would to my mind, pronounce itself to be incapable of undergoing the test of truth. It would say in effect, 'examine me not, for you will find me false.' " Wilberforce had averred that Christianity had "nothing to lose and all to gain from the fullest inquiry—if only it be humbly and faithfully conducted." But what, asks Smith, do you mean by "humble" and "faithful" inquiry? "Do you mean that the inquirer, in commencing his investigation, is not to contemplate the possibility of his arriving at any but one conclusion?"[17] Frederick Temple raised the same point in a letter to A. C. Tait: "To tell a man to study, and yet bind him under heavy penalties to come to the same conclusions with those who have not studied, is to mock him. If the conclusions are prescribed, the study is precluded."[18]

To men such as Goldwyn Smith and Ludlow and the authors of *Essays and Reviews*, it was the suppression of doubt and inquiry and not its admission that was subversive of belief and responsible for a lack of candor and truthfulness. "Conscientious doubt," wrote Smith, "when suppressed, eats into the soul like a cancer." The result is not true belief but "latent infidelity and the total corruption of the moral and spiritual nature."[19] For these men the evil of the age was "lazy beliefs in the easily credible."

*Essays and Reviews* caused unsettlement and indignation which led in turn to the book's denunciation by Convocation and legal proceedings against two of the authors, H. B. Wilson and Rowland Williams, on the grounds that their teachings contradicted the Articles of Religion. The two were sentenced to a year's suspension from their benefices by the Court of Arches but, on appeal, were acquitted by the Privy Council. The Council's verdict was a landmark for, as Arthur Stanley remarked, the latitude of interpretation now sanctioned meant that henceforth the matter of subscription was thrown back upon the individual conscience. In fact, however, the court's action newly underlined the confusion over subscription. Depending on one's viewpoint, the present assent was either needlessly exact and harrassing or shamelessly vague and ineffectual. New calls went out for, if not abolition, a modification and relaxation of the terms of subscription. Lord Ebury's bill, introduced to the Parliament in 1863, called for a simplifying of the clerical declaration, but the bill was defeated by the concerted opposition of Archbishop Langley and a majority of the bishops.

The defeat provoked a pamphlet war. Two of the ablest defenders of relaxation were Arthur Stanley and A. C. Tait. Both men directed attention to the pernicious effect the present subscription had on the minds and consciences of young men. In "A Letter to the Lord Bishop of London on the State of Subscription in the Church of England," Stanley pointed out that Jeremy Bentham's subscription as an undergraduate had "left a stain upon his conscience which was never effaced in after life."[20] "We must express our conviction," Stanley continued, "that the imposition of subscription, in the manner in which it is now imposed in the University of Oxford, habituates the mind to give a careless assent to truths which it has never considered and naturally leads to sophistry in the interpretation of solemn obligations."[21]

The gulf which separated the Anglican clergy on this issue is indicated by the following appraisals of the situation at the time. One bishop, in his address to Convocation, warned that "the effect of a relaxing of subscription must be disastrous. The faith of the people in the honesty of the clergy will be disturbed. The laity will think the clergy read prayers in which they do not believe and the moment that occurs all honest and right-minded men will, if they have any sense of Christian morality, leave the Church."[22] Frederick Temple, in a matter of years raised to the Primacy of the Church of England, perceived the issue quite otherwise. Adherence to the old forms of assent were, on the contrary, driving conscientious men out of the ministry, "the inevitable result (being) to poison the minds of the laity with the suspicion that the clergymen who remain teach what they do, not because they believe it, but because they fear the fate of their brethren."[23]

On the urging of Bishop Tait, a Royal Commission was appointed to study the subject of clerical subscription and, despite the heat of controversy, concluded its work with a unanimous recommendation for the simplification and relaxation of the forms of assent. On May 19, 1865, the Commission's will was given legislative effect in the House of Commons by passage into law. In lieu of "unfeigned assent and consent to all and everything" within the Prayer Book, clergymen now were to declare a general "assent to the Thirty-nine Articles of Religion and to the Book of Common Prayer" and to affirm belief in "the doctrine of the Church of England as therein set forth to be agreeable to the Word of God."

While the nettle of subscription appeared to have been firmly grasped, the advantage of such an action was not apparent to many thoughtful men. Arthur Stanley's sanguine prophecy that after 1865 the controversy would wane did not prove true. The issue remained whether the latitude implied in the decision of the Privy Council in the cases of Wilson and Williams and the Subscription Act of 1865 would not allow clergy to disguise their disbelief under the cloak of either a legal vagueness or general assent.

There were, in fact, many of the Board Church school who defended the right of the clergy to recognize the legal interpretation as the legitimate bounds of their subscription. One such was H. B. Wilson, who had urged such a view in his essay on "The National Church." "A great restraint is supposed to be imposed upon the clergy by reason of their subscription to the Thirty-nine Articles," wrote Wilson. "Yet it is more difficult than might be expected to define what is the extent of the legal obligation of those who sign them; and in this case the strictly legal obligation is the measure of the moral one." The act of subscription didn't amount to more, in Wilson's judgment, "than an acceptance of the Articles of the Church as the formal law to which the subscriber is in some sense subject."[24]

The position taken by men like Wilson was demoralizing to many, especially when it was publicly recommended by bishops in the House of Lords and at Church Congresses.[25] It could not, however, be held to represent the Broad Church position, which varied widely. Rowland Williams, co-defendant with Wilson before the Court of Arches, repudiated the notion that the legal obligation is the measure of the moral one. He wrote to his Counsel James Fitzjames Stephen requesting that it be made known that he was "by no means satisfied with the principle laid down by an eminent Bishop in the House of Lords, that subscription to the Articles means mere conformity to the Church. Signature of propositions appears to the Defendant to imply belief in what is signed."[26] Williams would not, he vowed, have been ordained had he not believed in good faith that to which he had given assent. In a letter to the Lord Bishop of Salisbury, Williams expressed his distress at being identified with the legal position on assent. "It has been a personal subject of uneasiness to me," he wrote, "to observe that some writers ... have a habit of harping on my name ... as if it were, or ever had been, a desirable object with me to evade, by any kind of legal process, the just degrees of stringency inherent in our Church formularies."[27]

Tractarians and Evangelicals alike were depressed by the decision of the Privy Council in the cases of Wilson and Williams, since sacred matters of the Church's faith and order were adjudicated by a predominantly secular court. Pusey wrote indignantly against the Council's decision and its authority, demanding that the bishops be entrusted with the function of "declaring what is the faith of the Church" *with judicial authority*.[28] Others, principally the Bishops of Salisbury and Oxford, proposed that the Council's actions not be sanctioned by the Church through exclusion of bishops from the Judicial Committee. The Tractarian opposition to the Court's decision had to do with the Court's willingness to acknowledge that a "non-natural" sense might be put on the words of the Articles and Prayer Book. Pusey wrote to Gladstone of the "utterly unprincipled Judgment" which allows "a non-natural sense might be put on every doctrinal term."[29] Keble likewise wrote to *The Times* decrying the ruling whereby "a theological word is not to be taken in its known theological sense . . ."[30]

The central issue here, of course, was begged and it was soon pointed out. Williams' counsel, Fitzjames Stephen, devastated the notion of a simple natural sense in the use of such theological terms as "everlasting," "justification," and "inspiration." "It is the fundamental weakness of most theological writers," Stephen wrote, "that they seem not to have any conception of the degree of precision of language which is required for the purpose of precluding discussion." Theologians are all too ready "to impute to all who differ from them any conceivable degree of treachery and dishonesty"[31] rather than admit that the formularies are to a large extent indefinite.

Stephen points up the effect of turning over the legal judication to the bishops:

> The immediate consequence would be that there would be no such thing as open questions on points of doctrine within the Church of England. Whenever a controversy arose, either or both of the controversialists could prosecute their opponents and the court would have to define the doctrine of the church upon the subject . . . The effect would be to give force of law to the current opinion of the clergy.[32]

Stephen was one with his defendant Rowland Williams in holding that the moral obligations of the clergy were untouched by the legal decisions:

> Nothing has been said or done which even implies that Dr. Williams or Mr. Wilson have not been guilty of a great sin in writing what they have written. All that has been decided is, that they are not liable to legal penalties for it. What then is the cause of this outcry? It can only be caused by distrust of the operation of those moral sanctions to which Mr. Pusey so powerfully appeals.[33]

While few still held that penal proceedings against errant clergymen were the best way to insure the Church's truth, few also were as assured of the beneficial effect of a latitudinarian assent, as was Stephen. Men of widely different schools saw the events of 1864-65 as having a corrupting influence. Gladstone wrote that "the general tendency and effect of the judgments has been and is likely to be hostile to definite teaching, and unfavorable also to the moral tone and truthfulness of men who may naturally enough be tempted to shelter themselves under judicial glosses in opposition to the plain meaning of the words."[34] But what concerned many thoughtful persons was not the possible dishonesty and equivocation of the men who held doctrines seemingly incompatible with their verbal professions; such an imputation of unveracity was, after all, pretentious and unjust. What bothered these persons was the false appearance and misrepresentation that the wide assent encouraged in the clergy's conduct of public worship. "The law may say," wrote Leslie Stephen, "that by professing a belief in the canonical scriptures, I only imply a modified belief in an uncertain part of them. But a man may feel that by using such words he is conveying a false impression to his hearers, and is propagating a doctrine from which he inwardly revolts."[35] Stephen believed a man may have many obligations but certainly foremost was the duty of not taking part in the spread of error and superstition.

Henry Sidgwick took a similar view. He could not follow many of his liberal friends in taking shelter under the broad legal interpretation. Distressed that his friend T. H. Green was considering taking orders as a deacon due to the relaxed subscription, Sidgwick could only lay it to the dilatory "milieu of Oxford that a high-minded man could think of it."[36] Sidgwick confessed to Mrs. Arthur Clough that it was his "painful conviction that the prevailing lax subscription is not perfectly conscientious in the case of many subscribers" but, worse, "that those who subscribe laxly from the highest motives are responsible for the degradation of the moral and religious feeling that others suffer."[37]

Sidgwick was repelled by the prospect of being an accomplice in such moral turpitude and resigned his Fellowship at Trinity College in June, 1869. What most caused Sidgwick to pause before taking this action was not doubt about the rightness of his own personal decision but that his example would force him "to condemn others for not acting in the same way," for "a moral impulse must be universally legislative."[38]

Most men who found themselves in disagreement with the formularies considered their differences of no religious importance and thus could hardly be expected to excommunicate themselves. No objection could be made to such a stance *if*, Sidgwick maintained, the indifference is understood on both sides. But this is usually not the case and certainly should not be assumed. The gap between the traditional sense and the new interpretation is often so wide as to approximate opposites! "It is much pleasanter," writes Stephen, "to say that we believe in everlasting punishment but that everlasting punishment means nothing that can shock the most humane mind, than to denounce the doctrine as untrue."[39]

According to both Stephen and Sidgwick "the duty of making his position clear rests with the divergent." The cleric has a responsibility not only to himself but to his auditors. The rule of veracity of speech involves every effort to make one's meaning plain. Sidgwick observed that "there is no danger to religion which the earnest person more deplores and dreads than there should insinuate itself into his religious exercises a sense of their shallowness and unreality; a feeling that the view of the universe which they are framed to suit is not precisely that which his innermost self actually takes."[40] That is to use language in a way incongruent with its common use and acceptance. This rule is not to deny a possible latitude of meanings; it implies only that the new meaning be one which the words will fairly bear. However, Sidgwick concludes, "where this new meaning cannot be imparted without violent straining of language, it seems to me less troublesome, and certainly not more injurious to our habits of sincerity, to admit that the words have become meaningless to the speaker."[41].

Stephen offered a simple test for judging acceptable bounds of meaning allowed in religous discourse:

> Let a man put out of his mind, as far as possible, all the old phrases with which he has become familiar, and simply express his thoughts in the clearest language he can find. If this new expression falls in naturally with the old, there is no more to be said. If there is a palpable difficulty in reconciling them, the problem occurs whether he shall use the old in a new sense, or simply abandon language perplexed with so many misleading associations?[42]

To Stephen the latter course was the only sincere one to take. If carried through, such action would be healthy all around and gain new respect for clerical integrity. It would, however, in many cases force the Anglican cleric to resign his office. He could not, for example, abandon belief in the Virgin Birth, hence language affirming it, and continue to recite the Creeds day in, day out. The clergy had no other choice, in Stephen's mind, as long as the church clung to the Articles and the Creeds.

Sidgwick was more sensitive to the complex motives that would cause a man to resist abandoning his ministerial office in the Church of England. He believed that the call for an educated ministry and a uniform belief and worship were essential but "an impossible combination." Sidgwick was thus unable to give any positive instruction to a church seeking to maintain just such a union. He agreed that during times of religious change and uncertainty "to say that during this period no one who was in favour of the change should perform the functions of the ministry, would be to lay down a rule so practically ruinous, that the most rigid moral theorist must recoil from it." But in his next breath he advises that advanced thinkers should not occupy the pulpits of the established church since "it seems to me impossible that a man can satisfactorily perform the functions of pastor if his opinions are not more or less in harmony with those of his flock."[43] Any kind of reserve is condemned; veracity of speech and intellectual sincerity are of paramount importance; but such as follow this moral path will find themselves outside the established church—or so Stephen and Sidgwick contended.

Men like Stephen and Sidgwick were troubled why others were not conscience-stricken to take action similar to their own, men of excellence who could not justly be charged with unveracity. The answer was, of course, that others calculated the moral loss and gain differently. Aware of the dangers of lax subscription in encouraging misrepresentation, hence erroneous belief and moral suspicion, these men saw in a vigorous and literal ethics of subscription a lack of historical sense and a bribe against scholarly inquiry, a dangerous theological complacency ultimately injurious to the church's mission. To opt out of the church would be to fail morally to assist in that mission.

Many Broad churchmen believed that Stephen sorely missed the mark when he pronounced that one must decide "which duty is just now the most important: to speak out with the utmost clearness, or to keep the Church of England together a little longer."[44] If these were the real alternatives, the vast majority of Liberals would unhesitatingly have stood with Stephen in insisting that "the one duty . . . of paramount importance is the duty of perfect intellectual sincerity." There were few who were willing to hold the Church of England together by intentional deceit.

The problem for most of the progressive clergy was how to steer a way between an excessive reticence and concealment leading to suspicion of disingenuousness and moral insincerity and a forthright profession which might well cause acrimony and division—and perhaps needless loss of office. The call for a middle way was well expressed by William Knight:

> We are no more called to announce to all and sundry how far we agree and how far we differ from them, than to be inquisitive about our neighbor's faith, and with regular curiosity or selfishness to strive to be his conscience keeper. Such procedure would engender a miserable egoism, and the ceaseless obtrusion of one man's idiosyncracies . . . upon the notice of others. It is true that no one is at liberty to cloak or conceal his opinion from indolent acquiescence, or a desire for 'peace at any price,' but it is enough if he lets his convictions find utterance when it is spontaneous and natural to do so; or when truth would be compromised by silence or reticence.[45]

Within these bounds no cleric, Knight argued, need feel a more scrupulous responsibility to inform his people of his particular dissent, such as Sidgwick implied. To Broad churchmen such as Knight it is up to the individual to determine whether or not his dissent becomes greater than his "general assent" will honestly allow. The church cannot expect a man to excommunicate himself over a doctrine he cannot think fundamental. The responsibility of excommunication in such cases must rest with the collective church:

> Is it to be supposed that a clergyman is bound, on the first discovery of an intellectual difference from his brethren, to withdraw from their society, to bring his labours amongst them to a close? . . . It is folly to assert it. For the process would be an endless one. If he is in search of an ideal church, with an ideal creed, he will find none upon the earth; and he will be like the knights errant in quest of the Holy Grail.[46]

The position taken by most of the progressive school of clergy was between that of Sidgwick and Stephen, who refused subscription, and that of men such as H. B. Wilson, who simply held the legal bounds to be the measure of the moral responsibility. This third position was based on several weighty considerations. First of all that, granting the necessity of doctrinal standards or efforts to articulate a community's beliefs, all standards are, nevertheless, but approximations of an adequate statement of the truth of what are transcendent, metaphysical realities. Secondly, that it is not possible for the same intellectual articulation (creed) to satisfy every mind within the church at any one time. Nor, thirdly, can it be assumed possible for any creed to remain an adequate expression of belief from one age to another. It is the very assumption of creedal perfection which serves to arrest theological inquiry, to "preclude study." This last point remained, as we shall see, the great barrier separating the Broad Church school from the Tractarian and Evangelical position on subscription.

The Liberals' insistence on avoiding expulsion from the church except at the personal cost of the most flagrant breach of honesty, was based additionally on the genuine conviction that reform of the church could not be achieved from a position outside that body. "It cannot be done by outsiders," insisted William Knight. "The church will not listen to the voice of reformers who stand outside its pale."[47] No less an eminence than J. S. Mill gave his support to the Broad Church view. Mill claimed it was right for men to remain in the church and seek to change her, whether or not they agreed with the generally received interpretations of the formularies, "so long as they are able to accept its articles and confessions in any sense . . . consistent with common honesty."[48]

It is interesting to note that Rowland Williams, marked by orthodox churchmen as no less than an arch-infidel, took a more rigorous position on this matter than many of his liberal colleagues. He stood with Sidgwick in his sensitivity to the responsibilities of the priest to speak candidly to his people. At the same time he felt strongly that clergy seeking to liberalize the church's doctrine from within had solemn obligations to respect the doctrinal standards of the church. He thus expressed his "regret that Mr. Mill has lent his high authority to the principle of innovation from within . . . without inquiring with what limitations it be also right."[49] Whoever would seek to make the Anglican Church Unitarian or Roman, for example, should, Williams insisted, "do his work outside, and has no ground of complaint if he is turned out."[50]

How then did Williams justify his own vigorous action on behalf of doctrinal liberalization from within the church, in view of an ethical view of subscription as scrupulous as that of Sidgwick? The answer to this question should shed considerable light on the often unrecognized but cardinal issue between men such as Dr. Williams and Bishop Wilberforce, and later between Bishop Gore and Hensley Henson — and help explain why the ethics of subscription was clouded by such pathetic misunderstanding.

The view which prevailed among moderate clergymen of all parties at the time is well expressed by C. E. Prichard. Yet it is obvious how irritatingly it begs the question for both Rowland Williams and Samuel Wilberforce:

> Now it is quite unavoidable that in this process (of separating the essentials of Christian belief from the non-essentials) many sincere Christians must appear to those in a less advanced stage to be parting with what is closely bound up with truth itself. Still it remains true that the great points of Christian faith are distinguished in a real and practical sense, by a broad line of demarcation.[51]

In fact, what constituted the great points of Christian faith was in profound dispute.

The pathos of the moderate position is illustrated in the Bishop of London's charge to his clergy in 1866 at the height of the controversy over the Clerical Subscription Act of 1865. Bishop Tait sought to allay the fears and demoralization of many of his clergy by assuring them that "the essentials of the Christian faith are incorporated in our formularies from the Bible and the Apostles Creed — explained and enlarged on but not added to" and that "the liberty of thought which is consistent with loyalty to our church is therefore hedged in by these essentials."[52]

How, one must ask, is liberty of thought hedged by "the essentials" if the Bible is the final court of appeal? There is an answer, one given by Evangelical and Tractarian alike. It was the answer of Wilberforce and of J. B. Mozley. Mozley opposed the relaxing of the terms of subscription and did so on the grounds of Biblical authority. He believed an obvious point had been overlooked in the debates over subscription. For wherever "the language of a doctrinal formulary and the language of Bible are the same, whatever explanation we give, in case there is a difficulty, of the language of the Bible, is applicable to the language of the formulary as well." Therefore, Mozley contends, "in such a case, the statement in the formulary is no fresh difficulty, but only one which we have already surmounted in accepting the same statement in the Bible."[53]

The question, of course, is what is involved in "accepting the same statement in the Bible?" Mozley could with equanimity conclude that "the whole brunt of the struggle has been borne by Scripture, and under the shelter of that intervening barrier the Articles recline in peace" — becuuse he held the biblical *text* to be divinely inspired. Mozley could claim the Articles and Creeds were "saved the exposure to the open sea of interpretation" because of the protective barrier of an inspired biblical text. The waves of interpretation, he wrote, "dash upon the rock of inspiration before they reach (the Articles), and having spent their force leave a comparative haven for exegesis."[54]

What is implied here is the notion of a plain, natural sense to the Articles which is, finally, enshrined in and insured by an inspired biblical text. To give way at this point appeared to open the gates to the final triumph of non-natural senses and hence to the position that the church's standard could mean all things to all men. Gladstone's objection "to non-natural senses in general"[55] was widely shared. But was the notion of a plain natural sense, admirable as it might be ideally, possible or even honest for a genuine inquirer in such a period of scholarly theological transition? Surely Leslie Stephen's unequivocal demand for plain-speaking and Mozley's appeal to an inspired text were simplistic and lacking in historical sense. Rowland Williams could neither adopt Mozley's unhistorical doctrine of Scripture nor would he follow Sidgwick in resigning, though he agreed with Sidgwick's call for verbal candor and definiteness. Nor was he deceived by the tempting but illusory demand for a plain, natural statement of doctrine. He believed that scholarly honesty and forthright assent to the standards of the church were compatible and consistent with retention of his clerical office. This was so *because those standards found their warrant in Scripture whose meaning could best be ascertained by scholarship, which was ever open to new light.*

On this ground Williams could hold that no obligation as a clergyman could affect adversely his duties as a scholar nor his scholarship contradict his vows, if such "enquiry dealt righteously by the monuments of sacred literature." "By the act of Ordination a clergyman binds himself to study," he wrote, "and is responsible before Heaven for the task of bringing (the church's doctrines) into harmony with fresh facts and wider experience."[56] Williams believed this in no way involved disloyalty to the church.

> It is one thing to say we will never falsify sacred literature . . . while even the saying may be accompanied by the concession that a free development of Biblical research might logically lead up to modifications in our church system . . . but it would be a widely different thing to say, we owe no hearts allegiance, sympathy, belief, obedience, to the system, aspirations, doctrines, ritual, to which we are manifestly bound.[57]

Williams' position did not receive wide acceptance. It would appear that certain reputedly irreverent statements in his contribution to *Essays and Reviews* deafened his clerical colleagues to what else of value he had to say. But there is a deeper, more significant reason. Owen Chadwick has observed that in the famous Victorian argument over science and religion the real struggle did not concern their respective conclusions but more fundamentally "the right of the scholar to pursue his enquiries unhampered by non-scientific barriers."[58] This was the often hidden issue in the controversy over the ethics of subscription in the 1860's and early 1870's. As we shall see, it continued to be the underlying issue in the debate well into the second decade of this century.

[1] *Fortnightly Review*, N. S. XIV, (Dec. 1873), 74-2.

[2] L. Huxley, *Life and Letters of T. H. Huxley*, I, (London, 1900), 217.

[3] J. W. Cross, *Life and Letters of George Eliot*, I, (London, 1885), 103. I am indebted to Noel Annan's *Leslie Stephen* for statements of Newman, Huxley and Eliot.

[4] H. P. Liddon, *Life of E. B. Pusey*, II, 286.

[5] *Macmillan's Magazine*, (Jan., 1864), p. 216.

[6] *Apologia*, Longmans Edition, New York, 1947, p. 366.

[7] While it is true that this was the immediate cause for Newman's writing the *Apologia*, there was an older and larger issue which had to do with charges against the veracity of the Roman Church and its clergy. There had been a long-standing polemic in England against Roman casuistry. It is reflected in Kingsley's original slur in the *Macmillan's* review. It is also evident in "What, Then, Does Mr. Newman Mean?" There he speaks of "those permissions to deception, which may be seen and formalized and detailed in the works of the Romish casuists . . . whose books have received the public and solemn sanction of the Roman see "(*Apologia*, Oxford Edition, London, 1913, p. 34). Kingsley's ablest defender in the debate with Newman, F. H. Meyrick, had earlier published a critique of Roman casuistry and truthfulness entitled "Alfonso

de Liguori's Theory of Truthfulness" (London, 1855). Newman sought to clarify his own position vis-à-vis the Roman casuists' use of lying and equivocation in an extended note appended to the 1864 edition of the *Apologia*. In brief, he argued that Roman Catholics were not bound by the opinions of particular authorities in the Church. Cf. footnote (10) below.

⁸ Margot Asquith, *The Autobiography of Margot Asquith*, I, (London, 1920), 123; L. Huxley, *Life and Letters of Thomas Henry Huxley*, I (London, 1900), 226.

⁹ Cambridge University Library, Add. MS 4989. Cited in Josef L. Altholz, "Newman and History," *Victorian Studies*, VII (March, 1964), 292.

¹⁰ There is a striking absence of anything but a superficial treatment of these vigorous criticisms of Newman in the host of sympathetic studies of his life and thought.

One of the more acute defenses of Kingsley was that of F. H. Meyrick, whose work is very seldom mentioned in discussions of the Kingsley-Newman affair. Meyrick makes plain that Newman, as a Roman Catholic, could not simply repudiate the teachings of St. Alfonso de Liguori, the authoritative Roman casuist whose laxity of views involving equivocation in matters of speaking the truth was made much of by Kingsley. Newman cannot repudiate Liguori's teaching since, Meyrick argues, "St. Alfonso's morality is Rome's morality." Meyrick quotes authoritative statements to show that this is the case. Meyrick then asks Newman: "Now with the teachings of St. Alfonso before you . . . is it not boldness bordering on excess of courage to say 'Protestants think that the Catholic system, as such, leads to a lax observance of the rules of truth . . . I lament *their* mistake, but I bear it as I may?' Prove it first to be a mistake before you make public your resignation under it. You can only do this in two ways. You can 1) repudiate St. Alfonso's authority, or 2) justify his statements. You are bound to do one or the other." *But Isn't Kingsley Right After All? A Letter to the Rev. Dr. Newman from the Rev. F. Meyrick*, (London, 1864) pp. 9-11. For a recent defense of Kingsley see G. Egner, *Apologia pro Charles Kingsley* (London, 1969).

¹¹ *Subscription to Articles: Is it Truth, or a Mockery? Considered in Reference to Essays and Reviews*. By a Graduate of Oxford. (London, 1861), pp. 13, 9.

¹² *The Quarterly Review*, 109 (1861), 302.

¹³ "Aids to Faith," *The Quarterly Review*, 112 (1862), 451.

¹⁴ "Clerical Subscription," *The Quarterly Review*, 117 (1865), 463.

¹⁵ *Ibid.*

¹⁶ Goldwyn Smith, *The Suppression of Doubt Not Faith: A Letter to the Lord Bishop of Oxford on His Two Sermons Entitled 'The Revelation of God and the Probation of Man'* (Oxford, 1861), p. 3. For the criticisms of Ludlow and Maurice see *Tracts for Priests and People*, (Cambridge 1861-62). Ludlow wrote "A Dialogue on Doubt" and Maurice's essay is entitled "The Mote and the Beam," in which, characteristically, he reminds the good Bishop that "God is the judge of moral honesty" and that He will require "from us all an account of our stewardship."

¹⁷ *Ibid.* p. 4.

¹⁸ R. T. Davidson and W. Benham, *The Life of A. C. Tait*, I (London 1891), 291. See also Tait's comments in his Visitation Charge to the clergy of London in 1862, pp. 6-11 (*Life*, I, 480f.). Tait had joined other Bishops in the condemnation of *Essays and Reviews* and received from Temple a sharp rebuke. Temple prefaced his remarks, quoted above, with a reminder that it was Tait who in earlier years had "urged us from the University pulpit to undertake the critical study of the Bible." A position similar to that of Temple's is taken by C. E. Prichard in *Thoughts on Free Inquiry, Evidences and Subscription* (London, 1864).

¹⁹ Goldwyn Smith, *op. cit.*, p. 12.

²⁰ A. P. Stanley, *A Letter to the Lord Bishop of London on the State of Subscription in the Church of England*, p. 24.

²¹ *Ibid.* p. 25.

²² *Chronicle of Convocation*, 1863, p. 1211.

²³ *Life of Tait*, I, *op. cit.*, 292.

²⁴ *Essays and Reviews* (London, 1860), p. 181.

[25] Henry Sidgwick wrote that "if by saying that the legal obligation is the measure of the moral one, it is meant that a man cannot be guilty of having broken an engagement unless he can be convicted by a Court of having done so, the principle is hardly one which we can wish the guardians of social morality to maintain." *The Ethics of Conformity and Subscription* (London, 1870) p. 35.

[26] Rowland Williams, *Hints to my Counsel in the Court of Arches*, (London, 1861-62) pp. 17-18.

[27] *Life and Letters of Rowland Williams*. Edited by His Wife. II, (London, 1874). 265. In a letter of Sept. 25, 1866, Williams writes: "So-and-so showed me a paper by _____ for the Norwich Congress on the liberty of the clergy. It was written in that vile destructive spirit of evading religious obligation and profiting by legal evasion . . ." *Life, op. cit.*, 264. Leslie Stephen was quite wrong when, in his important essay on "The Broad Church," he wrote that "the theory of the Broad Church party is that the legal restrictions upon the clergy are the measure of the moral restrictions." (*Fraser's Magazine*, March 1870) This was the position of some, but by no means all, Broad Churchmen.

[28] *Case, As to the Legal Force of the Judgment of the Privy Council in re Fendall vs. Wilson . . . and a preface to those who love God and His truth*. (Oxford, 1864).

[29] Letter of Feb. 18, 1864. H. P. Liddon, *Life of E. B. Pusey*, IV (London, 1897), 83.

[30] Cited in Liddon, *op. cit.*, p. 91.

[31] J. F. Stephen, "Dr. Pusey and the Court of Appeal," *Fraser's Magazine*, Nov., 1864, p. 648.

[32] *Ibid.*, pp. 649, 650.

[33] *Ibid.*, p. 653.

[34] Letter to Sir W. Farquhar. John Morley, *Life of Gladstone*, II, (London 1903), 165.

[35] Leslie Stephen, "The Broad Church," in *Essays on Freethinking and Plainspeaking* (London, 1893), pp. 5-6.

[36] *Henry Sidgwick: A Memoir*. Ed. A. Sidgwick, (London, 1906), p. 105.

[37] *Ibid.* pp. 200-201.

[38] *Ibid.* p. 199.

[39] Leslie Stephen, *Essays.*, p. 38.

[40] Henry Sidgwick, *Ethics of Conformity and Subscription*, p. 27.

[41] *Ibid.* p. 31.

[42] Leslie Stephen, *Essays.*, p. 36.

[43] Henry Sidgwick, *Ethics of Conformity and Subscription*, pp. 28-29.

[44] Stephen, *Essays*, p. 36.

[45] William Knight "The Ethics of Creed-Subscription," *Contemporary Review*, 20 (1872), 332.

[46] *Ibid.* p. 333.

[47] *Ibid.* p. 334.

[48] Cited in F. W. Cornish, *History of the English Church in the Nineteenth Century*, Part II (London, 1910), 216.

[49] Rowland Williams, "On the Theory of Clerical Obligation," *Fortnightly Review*, (March 1868), p. 264.

[50] *Ibid.*

[51] C. E. Prichard, *Thoughts on Free Inquiry, Evidences and Subscription* (London, 1864), p. 13.

[52] *Life of Tait*, I, 483.

[53] J. B. Mozley, *Subscription to the Articles. A Letter to the Rev. Professor Stanley* (Oxford, 1863), pp. 4-5.

[54] *Ibid.*, p. 24.

[55] *Life of Gladstone*, II, 165.

[56] Rowland Williams, *Hints to my Counsel*, p. 13.

[57] *Life and Letters of Rowland Williams*, II, 266-67.

[58] Owen Chadwick, *Freedom and the Historian* (Cambridge, 1968), p. 27.

## II

The tension and conflict produced by the Victorian commitment to critical reason, coupled with a deeply-felt religious sensibility, reached its apogee in England in the 1870's, the period referred to by Basil Willey as "the classic decade of Victorian rationalism." The decade witnessed a considerable widening of the discussion of the morality of belief, beyond the issues of clerical subscription and ordination vows. A vigorous philosophical debate on the ethics of religious belief was sustained throughout the decade in the meetings of the Metaphysical Society and in the leading periodicals of the day by many of the most eminent late Victorian writers. The debate focused on the *ethics* of belief, since it was concerned not only with the logic of belief, the question of appropriate modes of inquiry or valid evidence, but with the morality of belief, the question of the sincerity and candor of believers. However, in the 1870's the latter question was seldom debated in isolation from the former; indeed, the two questions were, unfortunately, often confused and cannot easily be disjoined. These issues were not the subject of mere abstract analysis. For men like Newman, Sidgwick and Stephen they were matters of the most immediate, personal concern.

It is often remarked that the tension, and even fracture, brought about by the conflict in England between belief and science is symbolized in, and can perhaps be traced back to, the seminal influence of two great minds: Bentham and Coleridge. J. S. Mill described the unique contribution of the two as follows:

> By Bentham . . . men have been led to ask themselves in regard to any ancient or received opinion, Is it true? and by Coleridge, What is the meaning of it? The one took his stand outside the received opinion, and surveyed it as an entire stranger to it: the other looked at it from within, and endeavored to see it with the eyes of a believer in it . . .[2]

Mill concluded that "it was likely that each would find, or show the way to finding, much of what the other missed."[3] If they showed the way, few Victorians were able to resolve the dual vision. As we know, many eminent figures—Tennyson, Sidgwick and Arthur Clough, for example—agonized over the choice between these two intellectual traditions. They could choose neither side, nor were they able to reconcile satisfactorily the two positions. They remained caught on the horns of a dilemma.

The greater number of Victorian thinkers found themselves in the line of intellectual inheritance traceable to either one or other of the "two seminal minds." As Leslie Stephen remarked, "the same years saw the incubation of (Mill's) *System of Logic* and (Newman's) theory of Development." The Coleridgean line, which John Coulson calls "the fiduciary use of language," runs from Julius Hare in Cambridge and Thomas Arnold in Oxford through F.D. Maurice and the Broad Church theology of the sixties to Matthew Arnold and on to the later writings of Walter Pater. Most importantly, Coleridge's ideas find remarkable parallels in Newman's *A Grammar of Assent*.[4] Newman's distinction between different kinds and motives of assent and his notion of the act of assent by means of a spiritual intuition — the illative sense — are reminiscent of Coleridge's doctrine.[5]

In the great debate over belief, evidence, and certitude, it was Newman who carried on the Coleridgean tradition of historical and intuitive thought — and whose works were most often cited by the "intuitionists" against the "empiricists" and freethinkers.

The other great tradition of English thought cited by Mill — that of Bentham — also had its line of disciples in the mid- and late-Victorian decades. The tradition can trace its inheritance through James Mill to his son, J.S. Mill, to Alexander Bain and the vocal and influential freethinkers and agnostics of the 70's and beyond — Fitzjames Stephen, Leslie Stephen, W. K. Clifford, T. H. Huxley, and John Morley. Just as the intuitionists of the 70's looked to Newman, so the empiricists looked to J. S. Mill — and specifically to his *A System of Logic*. It became, in the words of Leslie Stephen, "a kind of sacred book for students who claimed to be genuine Liberals. It gave the philosophical creed of an important section of the rising generation."[6]

What Mill's *Logic* stood for was opposition to "intuitionism".[7] The *Logic* supplied a "much-wanted textbook of the opposite doctrine — that which derives all knowledge from experience."[8] The method of inquiry that will yield truth, Mill argued, is reasoning inductively from particular cases to an inference or generalization.[9] And *the* presupposition of the inductive, experimental method is, Mill acknowledged, the uniformity of Nature.[10] We know Nature is uniform and that the scientific, experimental method is the only method of discovering Nature's truths — this was Mill's legacy to the freethinkers of the late Victorian age. Progress for them depended on this belief and this method in the overcoming of error. Since erroneous ideas were a barrier to progress, a man's beliefs were a matter of the highest ethical concern. Beliefs are not merely personal matters — they are, after all, "that upon which a man is prepared to act"[11] — beliefs have social consequences. So argued Clifford and Stephen and Huxley as they threw down the challenge to the "intuitionists" to examine the reasons for their beliefs and discard those founded on what they considered to be merely authoritative, congenial, or even merely useful.

The debate over the ethics of belief in the 70's produced some of the most provocative and important modern writing on the subject of belief. In the 70's alone these writings included Newman's *Grammar of Assent* (1870), Henry Sidgwick's *The Ethics of Conformity and Subscription* (1870), Mill's essay on *Theism* (1874), John Morley's *On Compromise* (1874), James Fitzjames Stephen's *Liberty, Equality, Fraternity* (1874), Leslie Stephen's *Essays on*

*Freethinking and Plainspeaking* (1873) and *An Agnostic's Apology* (these essays originally appeared in the *Fortnightly* during the 70's; the book was published in 1893), and the papers by Bagehot, T. H. Huxley, W. G. Ward, the Stephen brothers, R. H. Hutton, Froude, and others were read before the Metaphysical Society and reprinted in various periodicals during the decade.

The debate focused the question of religious belief on what was considered a revolutionary new *ethic* of belief. The ethic was actually not new, since it was found classically stated in John Locke, but the Stephens, Clifford, Froude, and Huxley made it the first principle of their credo and through their writings it became widely known and approved among the younger of the educated class. Locke had written that there was one unerring mark of the lover of truth:

> viz., the not entertaining any proposition with greater assurance than the proofs it is built upon will warrant. Whoever goes beyond this measure of assent, it is plain received not the truth in the love of it; loves not truth for truth's sake but for some other by-end.[12]

Newman had read deeply in Locke as an undergraduate. His influence is clear in Newman's strong empirical bent, his acute awareness of the limits of reason, and his near-contempt of syllogistic logic. But Locke's morality of belief also stung Newman's conscience by the fact that Newman could not agree with Locke's formulation of it as assent directly proportioned to evidence. A few years before writing the *Grammar*, Froude had written Newman that "even the highest attainable probability does not justify the mind in discarding the residuum of doubt," and went on to lecture him that to tip the balance on other than rational grounds "is distinctly an immoral use of faculties."[13] Newman wrote *A Grammar of Assent* in large measure to convince men like Froude that one can honestly "believe what you cannot absolutely prove."[14]

As is well known, the key to Newman's position, and that which set him apart from Locke and those who followed Locke's ethic of belief, was Newman's distinction between real assent and inference. By 1866 Newman had come to believe that it was wrong to begin inquiry into belief with the problem of certitude. "Certitude," he wrote in a memorandum, "is only a kind of assent — you should begin with contrasting assent and inference."[15] Locke had said that assent should be proportioned to the evidence. "It follows from this," writes Newman,

> . . . that assent becomes a kind of necessary shadow, following upon inference . . . it is never without some alloy of doubt, because inference in the concrete never reaches more than probability.[16]

To say that probabilities should never lead to certitude is, in Newman's view, a "pretentious axiom," unrelated to what actually goes on in the real world. There are many truths which cannot be demonstrated, yet which everyone unconditionally accepts. Locke himself could not hold consistently to the axiom that it is immoral to "carry our assent above the evidence that a proposition is true," or to have "a surplusage of assurance beyond the degrees of that evidence,"[17] when considering the real practices of mankind. Newman points out that Locke's realism and candor cause him to make significant exceptions to his own ethic of belief.[18]

According to Newman, conditional inferences can move to unconditional assent, through the cumulation and convergence of probabilities,[19] "probabilities too fine to avail separately, too subtle and circuitous to be converted into syllogisms, too numerous and various for such conversion."[20] Assent to such a convergence of probabilities is entirely reasonable but, for Newman, also certain and unconditional. Such certitude, Newman acknowledges, is "a mental state" not simply a quality of propositions, for

> in all concrete questions . . . it is not a passive impression made upon the mind from without . . . but . . . an active recognition of propositions as true, such as it is the duty of each individual himself to exercise at the bidding of reason. . . everyone who reasons is his own centre.[21]

For Newman concrete reasoning is not reducible to formal demonstration. The sole and final judgment of the validity of an inference in concrete matters is the illative sense, i.e., the power of inferring truth from converging lines of evidence, none of which separately would justify certitude, but all of which, taken together, do justify it. We can ask a man to examine again the evidence and his process of reasoning — beyond that it is difficult to go, since, finally, each man reasons from his own unique center.

The important point here is that for Newman such assent and certitude are not only possible but *ethically right and imperative.* In the exact sciences we are justified in withholding our assent from evidences or conclusions that have not received demonstration. Such is not the case, in Newman's view, and here he stands with Kierkegaard and William James, when the issues are of an ultimate and moral nature, which demand action and whose truth is not finally reducible to a common assessment or judgment — what he calls "the logic of words."

Newman's *Grammar* was the fullest and ablest critique of the Lockean ethic of belief, newly advanced by the Victorian free-thinkers. The *Grammar* thus proved to be the touchstone of the debate over belief that consumed so many meetings of the Metaphysical Society and so many pages of the journals during the 1870's. Newman was not a member of the Society, but his doctrine of belief was ably defended by those in the Society sympathetic to his position — especially by William George Ward and R. H. Hutton. Ward, the editor of *The Dublin Review* and zealous Catholic apologist, who had preceded Newman into the Roman Communion in September 1845, was the ablest philosophical spokesman of the "intuitionist" position during this period. His logical acumen was greatly admired by J. S. Mill. Late in 1869 he presented a paper before the Society, "On Memory as an Intuitive Faculty." R. H. Hutton remarked that it "fell like a bombshell among the antagonists of intuitive certainty." Ward was convinced that the religious belief of his day needed a subtle investigation of the ethical element in conviction and the principles warranted by man's moral nature. One thing blocked such an undertaking: the assumptions of the empirical school of freethinkers. If one could establish the mind's power to perceive objective truth by intuition, one could disprove the fundamental assumption of empirical philosophy. The roadblock would be removed. Ward pressed home what he regarded as the crucial issue, viz., memory.

Phenomenalists say there are no intuitive truths to be assumed, "but they must still ascribe to (man) that intuitional faculty which is called *memory*," i.e., the belief that man is so wonderfully endowed that one can assume that in every case his clear impression of something as past corresponds with a past fact. "You find fault," Ward complains of the empiricists, "with objectivists for gratuitously and arbitrarily assuming first principles: was there ever a more gratuitously and arbitrarily assumed first principle than your own?"[22] Huxley had asserted (*Lay Sermons*, 359) that one can trust the present act of memory because in innumerable past cases the avouchments of memory have been true. But, Ward replies, "How do you know? . . . Professor Huxley cannot legitimately even guess that *anything whatever* has been 'verified by experience' unless he *first* knows that certain acts of memory testify truly."[23] Such certitude is, Ward argues, intuitive, by which he means "a primary truth which the human intellect is necessitated by its constitution to accept with certitude not as inferences from other truths."[24]

Ward did not have to wait more than a few months for the delicate investigation of the ethical element in conviction for which he called. Newman's *Grammar* served the purpose well. Ward expressed his admiration for Newman's work in an essay on "Certitude in Religious Assent" in the *Dublin Review* in April 1871. He follows Newman in attacking what he calls "equationism," i.e., the Lockean principle which enjoins the moral obligation of effecting an "equation" between the strength of one's conviction and the amount of proof on which it rests. Ward gives two answers to the equationist doctrine: Firstly, there are no *degrees* of certitude; consequently, when complete certitude is obtained, additional proofs can add nothing to one's conviction. Ward argues, for instance, that by the time he was twenty-five years old,

I possessed abundantly sufficient ground for complete certitude that there are such cities in the world as Paris and Vienna. Since that date, my *proofs* for this conclusion have much more than doubled; but it is simply ludicrous to say, that I should now be more than twice as certain of the fact as I was then; and I cannot be *more* than completely certain of it now.[55]

Secondly, Ward argues, men's strongest, most important, and reasonable convictions rest on implicit premises. He illustrates his point by his belief that Paris and Vienna exist and that his father is a man of spotless integrity.

In either case premiss has for years succeeded premiss, each leaving its legitimate impression on my mind and then forgotten. How is it possible that I can labour to equate my conviction with its evidence when that evidence, in its original and adequate shape, is

wholly inaccessible, having left behind it but a vague record on my memory . . . It is a
rather hopeless task certainly for the thinker to aim at proportioning his conviction to its
premisses; when these premisses, in their original and adequate shape are no longer present
to his mind.[26]

Further, even when one's premises are actually before him, they very often
defy his power of analysis. Newman had spoken of this when he said that

the mind (is) unequal to a complete analysis of the motives which carry it to a particular
conclusion, and is swayed and determined by a body of proof, *which it recognizes only as a
body, and not in its constituent parts.*[27]

To the disciples of Mill's *Logic* these arguments for religious certitude
newly put forward by Newman, Ward, and Hutton were immoral for, in their
opinion, they converted probabilities and strong feelings into evidence of facts
and unconditional certitude. As Fitzjames Stephen complained, they
increased "the bulk and weight of evidence by heating it with love."[28] Stephen
was one of the most intrepid critics of the religious belief of his day and
produced some of the sharpest and most telling arguments against the
Newman-Ward ethic of belief. The inheritance of an evangelical conscience
would not allow him to bide any compromise with an honest admission of
agnosticism in religious belief. He abhorred any creed held on grounds of its
antiquity or beauty or utility rather than on the grounds of its demonstrable
truth. To propose beliefs on any other grounds than rational evidence, he said,
"is like keeping a corpse above ground because it was the dearest and most
beloved of all objects when it was alive."[29]

In January 1872, Stephen published a critique of Ward entitled "On
Certitude in Religious Assent."[30] What Stephen found most unacceptable in
the Newmanian ethic was its notion of the absoluteness of certitude and its
rejection of Locke's degrees of assent. For Stephen all belief, even absolute
belief, is susceptible to degrees of stability for, while unaccompanied by
present doubt, such absolute assurance is consistent with the consciousness of
the possibility of future disconfirmation and doubt. Stephen finds Ward's first
argument, viz., that "there are no *degrees* of certitude," wanting. All belief, he
argues, admits to degrees of stability.[31]

Concerning Ward's second argument, Stephen acknowledged the validity
of implicit reasoning in which there is no articulate equation between
conviction and proof. He contends, however, that Ward does not recognize
the true basis of our assent to such reasoning.

The question is not whether such evidence as this is of weight, *but whence its weight is
derived?* Is it to be believed because it is inarticulate, *or if and in so far as it is observed to
lead to the truth?* . . . In the case of the physician and the insurance office the confidence of
the board would depend upon their general opinion of the physician's skill. They would
have observed that he was usually right in such matters.[32] (italics added)

It is painfully common for people to be absolutely convinced, yet unable to
make explicit their reasons, and to be dead wrong.[33]

Stephen goes on to point out that there are many cases of belief which are a mixture of the effects of evidence and of temperament. It is to these cases, he contends, that Newman and Ward most appeal. Their approach goes something like this: The truth of Christianity can't be proven beyond a doubt but neither can it be disproven. There are, nevertheless, evidences which point to its truth and from these the "illative sense" draws a certitude. Stephen comments:

> If this were merely an obscure and peculiar way of saying, 'I think it probable that Christianity is true, and I am content to act upon that probability,' I, for one, should not have a word to say to the contrary. But it is something more than this. Dr. Newman's theory—and (Ward's) too. . . seem to me to be that a certain feeling in your own mind can produce an effect upon facts outside of you; that your certitude can convert a probability into a certainty; that is, can cause a given set of facts to fulfil conditions which they would not otherwise fulfil. It seems to me just as rational to say that if you saw an object through a mist, which might be either a man or a bush, your conviction that it was a man could make it into a man.[34]

To refuse to recognize a belief as merely probable because millions, including yourself, have believed it true and have acted on that belief is, in Stephen's judgment, the moral weakness of the man who does not like to be disturbed in matters on which he has decided.

In the second chapter of *A Grammar of Assent*, Newman dwelt at length on what he considered the difference between assenting to a proposition and assenting to the truth of a proposition and placed great weight on the moral propriety of belief in the latter, i.e., in the mysteries of the faith, such as the Incarnation and the Trinity. Fitzjames Stephen argued that this crucial distinction of Newman's conveyed a false impression of a similarity between two very different things. To assent to a proposition is mentally to assert its truth, but to assent to the truth of a proposition is to assert that words of which the meaning is not understood by the asserter mean something true to someone else. These are two entirely different operations. Newman has described assenting to the *truth* of a proposition as *implicit* belief and has led one to think that express belief and such implicit belief were but two species of the same genus belief.

In a paper read before the Metaphysical Society on 12 January 1875, entitled "On a Theory of Dr. Newman's as to Believing in Mysteries,"[35] Fitzjames Stephen focused on Newman's doctrine of implicit belief. "I maintain," he asserted, "that the act of believing an intelligible proposition to be true, and the act of trusting another person's assertion that an unintelligible statement is a true proposition, have so little in common that they ought not be called by the same name."[36] According to Stephen, the condition under which one should assent to the truth of words one cannot understand is the same as that which would induce us to place confidence in assertions which we are unable to verify by our own senses.

> It is the case in which you understand the method by which the unintelligible result is said to have obtained, and in which you can see that the result may have been attained by it, though it is out of your own power to see for yourself that such actually was the case.[37]

The argument, "he said it, therefore it is true," is worth little in Stephen's view "unless we are in a position to judge both of the motives and of the means of knowledge of the asserter and of the generic resemblance of the matter asserted to other matters of the same kind . . ."[38]

Newman's failure to logically distinguish assent to the truth of a statement and belief in the veracity of a person and the related issue of common evidence or criteria provoked the criticism not only of the freethinkers but of Newman's theological contemporaries. F. D. Maurice, in a review which reveals strikingly the differences in the two men, criticizes Newman for the mischief caused by his failure to distinguish belief in a person and assent to a proposition. Isn't it essential, Maurice asks, to distinguish

> between faith in the general character of the speaker, which years may have deepened instead of weakening, and assent to a certain proposition depending on evidences with which she may have been imperfectly acquainted?[39]

John Tulloch argued similarly. "The utmost confidence in our mother's veracity can be no guarantee of the accuracy of her botanical knowledge . . . While we trust her, she may be utterly mistaken."[40] Tulloch judged Locke's canon of belief to be a far safer guide than Newman's, arguing that

> if men are to reason at all, there must in the end be an appeal to some common canons of reasoning . . . That is to say, the testimony borne by any mind itself to the truth must be a testimony capable of being also felt and borne by other minds.[41]

Locke's ethic and Mill's canons of reasonable belief were most persistently defended against the "intuitionists" by Leslie Stephen, younger brother of Fitzjames. In 1877 Stephen wrote three long papers on the logic and morality of belief, in each case pitting Locke's doctrine against that of Newman.[42] Stephen's thesis is Locke's: belief must be proportioned to evidence which is open to or in the common possession of reasonable men.

According to Stephen, the burden of proof lies with the person who contends that his belief should be immune from such a common standard. To such a person he would say,

> If my belief ought to vary from the degree thus prescribed, in what way, and according to what laws, ought it to vary? And what do you mean by 'ought'? . . . If you mean that the variation is (morally) right, because it will secure greater conformity of belief to facts, you are virtually asserting that there is an extralogical faculty for arriving at the truth . . .[43]

some super-sensuous, super-inferential faculty which presents us with intuitive truths. Such a faculty was, of course, proposed by Newman in terms of the "illative sense" and the workings of implicit belief.

Stephen acknowledged that in his analysis of the "illative sense" Newman had come upon a genuine mental operation which went far in describing the method by which men are convinced and do believe, and that such a method is useful in discriminating between real and sham belief. In our contemporary parlance, Newman had written a profound phenomenology of belief, providing a brilliant analysis of the laws of belief but not the laws of *right* belief. In Stephen's judgment, Newman had written an account "of the methods by which men are convinced, not of the methods by which doctrines are proved."[44]

Stephen granted that there were many situations where absolute suspension of judgment was impossible and yet "where the grounds of conviction are too complex and delicate to be expressible in syllogistic form," and that in such circumstances we must judge by the testimony of what Newman called the "illative sense." However, in such circumstances the testimony is necessarily congruous with our already accepted beliefs and is therefore judged to be true. But what one person perceives to be congruous another will consider incongruous. As Stephen remarks, "there is no objective certainty, though there is subjective conviction."[45] Evidence of all kinds strikes people differently, according to their prepossessions, their rational capacities and so on, but this, Stephen asserts,

> is entirely irrelevant to the logical problem . . . When a man's mind is constituted in a certain way, and certain evidence is brought before him, it will inevitably produce a certain opinion . . . But it has no bearing upon the other question, whether a man's mind is rational, or whether he deals with the evidence in accordance with logical rules. Those rules simply express the conditions which secure a conformity between opinion and fact . . . a neglect of which leads a man into error.[46]

This is so because every religious system involves historical, philosophical, and scientific statements which can be compared with classes of facts which we know or believe on reasonable evidence to be true or probably true. Thus, Stephen argues, the judgment based on empirical tests which follow common logical rules is always to be given greater weight than that made by the "illative sense." He illustrates his point by reference to Newman's own example of discerning the authenticity of a passage of Shakespeare in terms of the character of its versification. Newman had made the point that we accept the word of the expert who pronounces judgment unhesitatingly on the basis of innumerable factors too delicate for him to put into words and of which he is not even himself conscious — rather than the judgment of the pedestrian syllable-counter. Stephen disagrees:

> A man with an exquisite intellectual taste can recognize the flavour of Shakespeare as distinctly as the epicure recognizes a special vintage, and may be as absolutely peremptory in his conclusions. Moreover, he can form a judgment upon matters where the humbler word-counter is hopelessly at a loss. His sphere of reasoning envelops and transcends that of his rival. *But his inference cannot be regarded as conclusively proved for anyone else.* We all know that critics are often peremptory in proportion to their ignorance. The counter of syllables, on the other hand, has proved beyond all doubt the fact which he asserts. There is undeniably such a likeness as he maintains, and in such a definite degree. The statement can be tested by every human being who possesses the faculty of counting,

and there is, therefore, no risk of a 'personal error'. It is convincing as far as it goes, not only to himself, but to the whole world of rational beings, and may take its place as a definite objective truth.[47]

Such a procedure is, Stephen argues, the only method of discerning the laws of right and, hence, morally justified belief.[48]

The intuitionists did not allow Stephen's critique to go unanswered. In an essay on "The Reasonable Basis of Certitude", W. G. Ward replied to Stephen's contention that Newman's *Grammar* is useful in discriminating between real and sham belief but not between true and false belief. "I think," writes Ward, "that he (Stephen) has not sufficiently remembered F. Newman's repeated inculcations of the doctrine that the laws of the human mind are in the last resort necessarily supreme arbiters of truth. Those judgments are self-evident, which the intellect avouches as such . . . for we cannot appeal from our faculties except by using those very faculties themselves."[49]*

R. H. Hutton also countered the thesis of Leslie Stephen's essay on "Belief and Evidence" in a paper read before the Metaphysical Society, entitled "On the Relation of Evidence to Conviction."[50] According to Hutton, evidence is only one legitimate ground of conviction. There are other causes

such, for example, as that 'pre-established harmony' between the nature of man and the external universe which, whether you ascribe it to intellectual, or moral, or spiritual instincts . . . or to other causes is, I believe, as potent a source of conviction, and of the kind of conviction that leads to wise action, as evidence itself.[51]

Stephen's Lockean demand that conviction should always be proportioned to the evidence needs so considerable a qualification and would leave our judgment in such a doubtful condition as to be, according to Hutton, for all practical purposes, worth little. Take Ward's case of memory:

If I do not misunderstand the drift of Mr. Stephen's paper, I have no right to this belief in the infallibility of my own memory, and ought to be decidedly more certain after I receive the full evidence, than I was before on the mere strength of that flash of the mind which assured me that I was remembering rightly.[52]

Hutton further contends that in all aspects of human life, beginning with memory and ascending to higher spheres of moral, aesthetic, and spiritual experience, there are trustworthy sources of conviction not founded on Stephen's notion of evidence. Take, for example, aesthetic experience:

The poet or artist is so by virtue of seeing, without evidence, and by virtue of the glance of his own higher faculty . . . When Wordsworth said to the girl who had climbed Helvellyn:

'Potent was the spell that bound thee,
    Not unwilling to obey
For the blue Aether's arms flung round thee
    Stilled the pantings of dismay.'

he had, I am quite sure, the deepest conviction that that very bold metaphor went to the heart of the feeling poured into the soul by the blue air on a mountain-top, and would recall that feeling to thousands of minds from which it had vanished. But assuredly neither of these convictions either were or could have been founded on evidence at all.[53]

Hutton does not deny that we often base our beliefs on false and vicious unreasoned assumptions as well as on true and salutary unreasoned assumptions. If the former can be refuted by evidence, all the better. But even in these cases, Hutton maintains, "it will be found to be true that it is quite as often not by intellectual evidence, but rather by the displacing influence of some larger and wider affection that they are undermined and removed."[54] We begin, Hutton argues, in almost every sphere of life from unevidenced convictions "which are as much part of the very moral stock-in-trade and capital of such a race as ours, as the pecuniary savings of one generation are the pecuniary capital of the next."[55] This instinctual or intuitive capital should mean that there is considerable fair presumption against allowing such a principle as Locke's canon to challenge the foundations of a society, "if for no other reason, still for this, that the effect of ages of belief surely ought to generate belief indefinitely stronger than any evidence the individual can command."[56]

In the mid 1870's the intuitionists were called upon to answer a relentless series of attacks on the logic and morality of their theory of religious knowledge. The severest and most provocative statement of the new morality of belief was made by W. K. Clifford before the Metaphysical Society on 11 April 1876. He entitled his paper "The Ethics of Belief."[57] While it lacked any consideration of the actual arguments of the intuitionists which marked the essays by Fitzjames and Leslie Stephen, it became, because of the simplicity of its rigorous principles, the classic statement of the new ethic of belief. According to Clifford, there is a moral duty of inquiry into belief no matter how trivial the matter, for the assent to beliefs prepares us to receive more of the same kind, and this weakens others.

If I let myself believe anything on insufficient evidence, there may be no great harm done by the mere belief; it may be true after all, or I may never have occasion to exhibit it in outward acts. But I cannot help doing this great harm towards Man, that I make myself credulous, and lose the habit of testing things, and inquiring into them. . . The credulous man is father to the liar and the cheat.[58]

If a man retorts that he has no time to study all the evidence and arguments and, moreover, would not be able to understand them, in any case — Clifford replies sharply: "Then he should have no time to believe."[59]

According to Clifford, the moral issue in belief "has to do with the origin of belief, not the matter of it . . . not whether it turned out to be true or false, but whether he had a right to believe on such evidence as was before him."[60] He gives as example the shipowner who firmly believes in the seaworthiness of his ship despite the fact that he fails to make the required inquiries and tests. The ship was, in fact, faulty, and went down, causing the death of the crew. "What shall we say of him?" asks Clifford.

Surely this that he was guilty of the death of those men. It is admitted that he did sincerely believe in the soundness of his ship, but sincerity of his conviction can in nowise help him, because *he had no right to believe on such evidence as was before him*. He had acquired his belief not by honestly earning it in patient investigation, but by stifling his doubts.[61]

Had the voyage ended without disaster, the shipowner's belief would still have been slothfully credulous and, therefore, morally wrong.

Often the simple excellence of a man's character is alleged as ground for assenting to his statements. On the contrary, replies Clifford,

> the goodness or greatness of a man do not justify us in accepting a belief upon the warrant of his authority, unless there are reasonable grounds for supposing that he knew the truth of what he was saying. And there can be no grounds for supposing that a man knows that which we, without ceasing to be men, could not be supposed to verify.[62]

Take, for example, the advice of a chemist:

> I have reasonable ground for supposing that he knows the truth of what he is saying, for although I am no chemist, I can be made to understand so much of the methods and processes of the science as makes it conceivable to me that, without ceasing to be a man, I might verify the statement . . . that the verification is within the reach of human appliances and powers.[63]

To the argument of Newman and Hutton and others that there is ethical warrant for belief in the consensus of the race, in the instinctive testimony of our ancestors accumulated over the centuries, Clifford replies that the answer is simple enough.

> The aggregate testimony of our neighbors is subject to the same conditions as the testimony of any one of them. Namely, we have no right to believe a thing true because everyone says so, unless there are good grounds for believing that some one person at least has the means of knowing what is true.[64]

For Clifford, as for others of the empiricist school, "the good grounds" of belief are to be found in Mill's principles of induction. Clifford acknowledged, with Mill, that every belief does go beyond experience (e.g., the child burned by fire yesterday avoids the flame today, *believing* it will burn her). "The question," Clifford asserts, "is not, 'May we believe what goes beyond experience?' . . . but 'How far and in what manner may we add to our experience in forming our beliefs?'" For Clifford the answer is clear:

> A burnt child dreads the fire. We may go beyond experience by assuming that what we do not know is like what we do know; or . . . we may add to our experience on the assumption of the uniformity of nature.[65]

What here appeared to the empiricists as an indisputable inference and canon of true belief appeared to many others, and not only the intuitionists, as a horrendous assumption, the Achilles heal of the empiricist argument. Henry Sidgwick, no intuitionist, attacked the empiricists at this very point in at least two papers read before the Metaphysical Society during this period.[66] Sidgwick commented that "one is amazed at the audacity of claiming a special trustworthiness for the intuitions of empirical psychology."[67] Mill himself, Sidgwick reminded his auditors, had acknowledged that the inference by which the uniformity of nature is obtained is not logically established and must be regarded as an hypothesis. "It appears," concludes Sidgwick, that a logical intuition relating to universal fact is admitted by the Empiricist . . . But if we are allowed the power of seeing universal truth in a single department of logic, on what ground is our natural claim to a similar faculty in other departments rejected?[68]

W. G. Ward, in an essay on "The Reasonable Basis of Certitude," in direct answer to both Clifford and Fitzjames Stephen, raised the same question of the empiricists as had Sidgwick—viz., what is the exact logical process by which one can reasonably satisfy oneself that nature proceeds universally on uniform laws? Ward was confident that the empiricist could give no answer.

Ward and several others regarded Clifford's rigorous ethic of belief to be not only founded on a vast metaphysical assumption but unreal and thus empty when considered in relation to common experience. Clifford had said that "no simplicity of mind, no obscurity of station," no belief "however seemingly trivial" could escape the duty of enquiry. Ward was quick to illustrate the absurdity of applying such rigor to all stations and circumstances: e.g., the belief in athletic victory based on local pride and *esprit de corps*, or beliefs of children and youth based on the word of their parents. In such cases to say that "the credulous man is father to the liar and the cheat" is nonsense.[69]

Ward points out that the philosophy of men like the Stephens, Huxley, and Clifford implies the theory "that the mind has only a power to criticize grounds of belief *independently* existing, and not itself to supply grounds of reasonable belief."[70] Referring once again to the case of memory, Ward asks:

What is the ground for knowing my experiences of ten minutes ago? What is the work of my intellect . . .? Is its work the arranging and marshalling grounds of belief external to the intellect itself? On the contrary . . . My only exclusive means of knowing with certitude the past fact of those experiences is the present avouchment of my intellect itself.[71]

Ward argues that there are cases similar to that of memory in which the mind itself supplies grounds of reasonable belief, viz., in the cognizance as self-evident of the various *a priori* synthetical judgments (as they were called by Kant) and in the workings of Newman's cumulative probabilities the mind pronounces a conclusion to be ascertained with absolute certitude.

R. H. Hutton joined in the attack on Clifford's challenge. He focused on the interesting point that the issue is not simply credulity or incredulity but the *motive* involved in either case. Incredulity can be as morally tainted as credulity. Hutton points to the weakness of Clifford's principal illustration of his point, viz., that of the shipowner:

The weak point of such illustrations is that the self-interest of the man is in this case engaged on the side of his credulity, and not against it,—a circumstance which should always put us morally on our guard against not only credulity, but incredulity, or any other attitude of mind which it would be for our own interest for us to assume. Put the case the other way. Your whole fortune is embarked in a given enterprise. Someone gives you most unwelcome but, on the surface, plausible information that the enterprise is hollow, and founded on a cheat. You know that if this be true you are ruined and also that if it be false, but be believed to be true, you are ruined by the panic which it will excite among others; it is therefore your *interest* to be incredulous, for by extinguishing the rumour at first you retain the chance of sustaining others' confidence, while if you give any credit to it, you create the panic by which others indeed may be saved, but you must be ruined. 'Incredulity', therefore, is the prompting of self-interest, and in such a case, incredulity is as wrong as Professor Clifford's credulity, and for the same reason. It is the tainted motive which makes the credulity and the incredulity alike evil.[72]

According to Hutton, Clifford's moral rule concerning belief has to do *not* with matters of pure credulity (e.g., Columbus' credulity concerning the location of Asia) but to acts of *interested* credulity.

At the beginning of the next decade, the new ethic of belief was examined by Wilfred Ward in one of the most thoughtful essays by a member of the intuitionist school.[73] Like Hutton, Ward focused on the *motive* of belief and on the cardinal importance of the *matter* of belief in consideration of the moral issue. Clifford and both Stephens had made much of the notion that "the wish is father to the thought," that feeling or wishing is prone "to put more into the evidence than there is in it." Ward contends, on the contrary, that the more we wish to believe in something which it is of great importance to us to find true, the less importance we attach to our wishes as affecting its truth. If, on the other hand, it is not of importance to us to know the truth, we can indulge our wishes and in such cases the wish is often father to the thought. Ward fashions his argument in a dialogue between the skeptical empiricist Darlington and his believing friend Walton.[74] According to Walton (Ward), "There are two very different states of mind — anxiety that something should be really true, and the wish to have the pleasure of believing something."[75]

Throughout the dialogue Darlington persists in his conviction that the believer is biased by his wish to believe. If two men of equal ability, one indifferent and the other anxious for religious belief, consider the evidence and the indifferent examiner finds it insufficient and the other is convinced, the latter is unreasonably biased by his wish. Walton disagrees, for, while the man's wish cannot put more into the evidence than is there, "it may make him find more than the other finds."[76] But even granted that the same evidence is before both men, "the religious-minded man may get beyond its logical statement; he will *feel* its force —." "Exactly," responds Darlington. "He will feel more than reason warrants." "No," persists Walton, "he does not substitute feeling; rather his feeling and his interest in the matter stir his reason to activity."[77]

Ward resorts to the illustration of two men judging the authenticity of a manuscript — an illustration used earlier by Newman and by both Stephens. Each man is faced with the same evidence, but one "has not," says Ward,

acquired that personal power which enables him to *weigh it truly* . . . Thus though the evidence might be similarly *stated* by both . . . each might give a similar list of arguments *pro* and *con* — the relative weight attached by them to this particular item would differ *toto caelo*. One grasps the full force of what the other only half understands.[78]

Ward concludes that in all evidence there are particular items which appeal differently to different individuals, without any want of candor in those making different assessments. R. H. Hutton, following Ward's lead, insisted further that differences of temperament affect judgments of evidence. Not, he claimed, that such differences in personality affect "the estimates formed of *particular evidence*; but that what it does affect is the choice of the evidence to which special attention is paid, and the choice of the evidence which is allowed to fall into the shade."[79]

Here, of course, we are back with Newman. Antecedent prepossessions, judgments, presumptions affect our perception of, for example, the nature and weight of common evidence. "Unbelief, indeed, considers itself especially rational, or critical of evidence," wrote Newman, "but it criticizes the evidence of Religion, only because it does not like it, and really goes upon presumptions and prejudices as much as Faith does, only presumptions of the opposite nature."[80]

Anticipating some existentialist motifs as well as important emphases in contemporary philosophical analysis, Newman stresses the role of intention and action in the life of belief. When we are not personally concerned, even the highest evidence does not move us; when we are concerned, the very slightest is enough.

The debate of the 1870's continued into the next decade and beyond — but the zealous positivism of men like Clifford failed to enlist vigorous new recruits. What Noel Annan has called "the curious strength of positivism" did not lose its hold on English thought, but it was challenged on many fronts. Influential men of letters and teachers like Matthew Arnold, T. H. Green and John and Edward Caird directed their considerable skills to opposing positivist empiricism and to establishing the warrants of religious belief on the solid ground of experience. Arnold mocked the literalistic criticisms of the Bible triumphantly paraded by the freethinkers. Such criticism lacked critical tact and historical sense. The Bible and the Creeds must not be viewed as scientific fact. They represent "language *thrown out* . . . concerning which, moreover, adequate statement is impossible."[81] Such "approximate" language is literary, the language of image, symbol and myth. Arnold sought to awaken his contemporaries to the fact that "the noblest races are those which know how to make the most serious use of poetry,"[82] for this language can often "cover more of what we seek to express than the language of literal fact and science. The language of science about it will be *below* what we feel to be the truth."[83]

T. H. Green sought to turn away the positivist assault in similar manner and, for many thoughtful people, with considerable success. For Green, as for Arnold, "the fair humanities of old religion" are gone forever. The old theology and its methods of proof are dead and yet "still the heart doth need a language." That language cannot be found in the assured results of scientific investigation of nature or history. "No deliverance indeed," writes Green, "is to be looked for from without."[84] Green insists that men cannot *find* a verification for their religious beliefs—they can only *make* them by means of experience. "Though the failing heart cries out for evidence, at the worst live on as if there were God and duty, and they will prove themselves to you in your life. The witness which God has given of Himself in the spiritual history of mankind you will in this way make your own."[85]

This is not far from Newman, and would have as little appeal to the followers of Mill. But what of Mill himself? He had been working on essays on religion during the sixties, but his *Three Essays on Religion* were published in 1874 only after his death. Much of what he wrote in the "Utility of Religion" and "Theism" dumbfounded and angered his disciples. Here Mill goes a long way toward embracing the position of Newman, Arnold, and Green. "To me," he writes,

> it seems that human life, small and confined as it is . . . stands greatly in need of any wider range and greater height of aspiration for itself and its destination, which the exercise of imagination can yield to it without running counter to the evidence of fact; and that it is a part of wisdom to make the most of any, even small, probabilities on this subject, which furnish imagination with any footing to support itself upon.

Mill adds "that it is possible to form a perfectly sober estimate of the evidences of both sides of a question and yet to let the imagination dwell by preference on those possibilities, which are at once the most comforting and the most improving . . ." Such a position, he concludes, "is legitimate and philosophically defensible."[86]

The philosophical tides were changing and Mill's essays on religion were a sign. William James was soon to publish his classic critique of the empiricists' dogma that "it is wrong, always, everywhere and for everyone, to believe anything upon insufficient evidence." To James, Clifford's charges of unveracity against the Christians, for holding beliefs on "insufficient evidence," cloaked the real issue. The evidence was sufficient; it was simply read the other way. The freethinkers "believe so completely in an anti-Christian order of the universe that there is no living option: Christianity is a dead hypothesis from the start."[87]

Here were criticisms sensitive to the deficiencies in the empiricist position but, nevertheless, one feels, circumventing rather than meeting Stephen and Clifford head on in the matter of what constitutes legitimate evidence of historical or factual beliefs. But looking back at the debate of the 1870's it is clear that both sides failed to meet directly their opponents' most persistent criticism. Both parties failed as well to make crucial distinctions and thus the debate was often muddled. The intuitionists failed, for example, to distinguish between the *act* of believing and *what* was believed, between moral or valuational beliefs ("believing in") and beliefs about matters of fact ("believing that"). The empiricists never answered to complete satisfaction the criticism of their rule governing belief (the uniformity of nature). Their metaphysical assumptions were exposed by the logicians Ward and Sidgwick and later by the Idealists and Pragmatists. The scrupulous rigor of their ethic of belief was

was shown by Hutton, the Wards and by James to be, when pushed to its logical end, a silly counsel of perfection, lacking existential relevance. The intuitionists were far more alert to the phenomenal facts of belief, recognizing the special importance of the matter and motive in cases both of credulity and incredulity. They saw the rightness of what William James called "self-verifying" beliefs, e.g., moral beliefs which actually change behavior so that it accords with the belief, hence are self-fulfilling. They were radical in their epistemological scepticism (in this respect the radical empiricism of the Newman tradition is one with the Kantian), and thus sensitive to the role of the personal agent in epistemological considerations.

It would appear that Mill was right: that Bentham and Coleridge "would show the way to finding much of what the other missed."

[1] *The Nineteenth Century*, 17 (1885), 485.

[2] *Mill on Bentham and Coleridge*, ed. F. R. Leavis, 1950, pp. 99-100

[3] *Ibid.*, p. 101.

[4] In *The Statesman's Manual* Coleridge had written: "It is a mystery: and we are bound to believe the words without presuming to enquire into the meaning of them. That is, we believe in St. Paul's veracity; and that is enough. Yet St. Paul repeatedly presses on his hearers that thoughtful perusal of the Sacred Writings, and those habits of earnest though humble enquiry which . . . would lead them 'to a full assurance of understanding (to an entire assent of the mind; to a spiritual intuition, or positive inward knowledge by experience)" pp. 56-57.

[5] Whether and how much Newman was directly influenced by Coleridge is much debated. For a recent citation of evidence indicating such an influence, see John Coulson, *Newman and the Common Tradition*, (Oxford, 1970), pp. 254-255.

[6] *The English Utilitarians*, III, (London, 1900), 76.

[7] In the *Autobiography* Mill wrote: "The notion that truths external to the mind may be known by intuition or consciousness independently of observation and experience is, I am persuaded, in these times the great intellectual support of false doctrines and bad institutions," pp. 225-226.

[8] *Ibid.*, p. 225.

[9] Induction is "that operation of the mind by which we infer that what we know to be true in a particular case or cases will be true in all cases which resemble the former in certain assignable respects." *A System of Logic*, 8th ed. (London, 1888), p. 210.

[10] *Ibid.*, p. 224.

[11] This is Alexander Bain's definition of belief.

[12] John Locke, *Essay Concerning Human Understanding*, II, (Oxford, 1894), 428-429.

[13] G. H. Harper, *Cardinal Newman and William Froude,* (Baltimore, 1933), p. 120.

[14] *Ibid.*

[15] Wilfred Ward, *The Life of John Henry Cardinal Newman*, II, (London, 1921), 278.

[16] J. H. Newman, *An Essay in Aid of a Grammar of Assent*, (Longmans: London, 1947), p. 120.

[17] Locke, *Essay, op. cit.*, p. 429; Newman, *op. cit.*, p. 123.

[18] "First he (Locke) says, in his chapter 'On Probability', 'Most of the propositions we think, reason, discourse, nay act upon, are such as we cannot have undoubted knowledge of their truth; yet some of them *border so near* upon certainty that we *make* no doubt at all about them, but *assent* to them *as firmly*, and act according to that assent as resolutely, *as if they were infallibly demonstrated*, and that our knowledge of them was perfect and certain.

"Again, he (Locke) says in his chapter on 'The Degrees of Assent', that 'when any particular thing, consonant to the constant observation of ourselves and others in the like case, comes attested by the concurrent reports of all that mention it, we receive it as easily, and build as firmly upon it, as if it were certain knowledge, and we reason and act thereupon, *with as little doubt as if it were perfect demonstration.*' And he repeats, "These probabilities rise so near to certainty, that they *govern our thoughts as absolutely* and influence our actions as fully as *the most evident demonstration.* Our belief thus grounded, rises to assurance." Newman, *op. cit.,* pp. 121-122; Locke, *op. cit.,* pp. 364, 375-376.

[19] Newman, *op. cit.,* p. 312.

[20] *Ibid.,* p. 219.

[21] *Ibid.,* p. 262.

[22] "The Rule and Motive of Certitude," in *Essays on the Philosophy of Theism,* I, (London, 1884), 3-4.

[23] *Ibid.,* p. 4.

[24] *Ibid.,* p. 6.

[25] "Certitude in Religious Assent," *The Dublin Review,* (April, 1871), p. 257.

[26] *Ibid.,* p. 258.

[27] *Ibid.,* p. 260.

[28] Sir James Fitzjames Stephen, *Liberty, Equality, and Fraternity,* (London, 1874), p. 344.

[29] Leslie Stephen, *The Life of Sir James Fitzjames Stephen,* (London, 1895), p. 370.

[30] *Fraser's Magazine,* January 1872.

[31] *Ibid.,* p. 28.

[32] *Ibid.,* p. 31.

[33] *Ibid.,* p. 32.

[34] *Ibid.,* p. 38.

[35] Printed copies of the Society's papers were distributed to members. A near-complete set of the Papers is in the possession of the Bodleian Library, Oxford.

[36] *Ibid.*

[37] *Ibid.*

[38] *Ibid.*

[39] "Dr. Newman's *Grammar of Assent,*" *The Contemporary Review,* 14, 1870, 156.

[40] "Dr. Newman's *Grammar of Assent,*" *Edinburgh Review,* CXXXII, 1870, 408.

[41] *Ibid.,* pp. 403, 407.

[42] "Belief and Evidence," a paper read before the Metaphysical Society, June 12, 1877, and "Newman's Theory of Belief," *The Fortnightly Review,* Nov. and Dec., 1877. The latter paper was reprinted in *An Agnostic's Apology.*

[43] "Belief and Evidence," pp. 2-3.

[44] "Newman's Theory of Belief," p. 209.

[45] *Ibid.,* 215, 216.

[46] *Ibid.,* p. 217.

[47] *Ibid.,* p. 212.

[48] A position similar to that of Leslie Stephen's was proposed by the historian James Anthony Froude in a paper on "Evidence" read before the Metaphysical Society on May 16, 1871. Froude set down his canon of belief as follows: "In every instance of a reported fact, we detract from the weight of the evidence the internal unlikelihood of the thing in itself. Where it is at variance with an experience which is otherwise uniform, the unlikelihood is at its highest, and where an historical event of such a kind is alleged to have taken place a long time ago, where the witnesses cannot be cross-questioned or the circumstances otherwise examined into, I maintain that an implicit acquiescence in the truth of such a story is illegitimate, *and so far as it is allowed to influence our conduct, is immoral,*" "Evidence," p. 3.

[49] *The Nineteenth Century,* March, 1877, p. 539. * Here Ward is reminding his readers of his essay "On Memory as an Intuitive Faculty" in which he speaks of memory as a "law" of the human mind, in that we can be certain intuitively that a clear impression of something as past corresponds to a past fact. It appears that for Ward a comparable faculty or power of the mind is Newman's illative sense.

[50] Read on Nov. 13, 1877.

[51] "On the Relation of Evidence to Conviction," p. 1.

[52] *Ibid.*, p. 3.

[53] *Ibid.*, p. 5.

[54] *Ibid.*, p. 6.

[55] *Ibid.*

[56] *Ibid.*, p. 7.

[57] The paper was published in *The Contemporary Review*, XXIX, 1877, to which we will refer below.

[58] "The Ethics of Belief," p. 294.

[59] *Ibid.*, p. 295.

[60] *Ibid.*, p. 290.

[61] *Ibid.*, pp. 289-290.

[62] *Ibid.*, p. 300.

[63] *Ibid.*, p. 301.

[64] *Ibid.*, p. 303.

[65] *Ibid.*, p. 306.

[66] "The Verification of Beliefs," April 27, 1870, and "The Incoherence of Empirical Philosophy," January 14, 1879.

[67] "The Verification of Beliefs," *The Contemporary Review*, XVII, 1871, 589.

[68] *Ibid.*, p. 590.

[69] Clifford had acknowledged that society could not permit persons to delay all recognition of the authority of certain moral commonplaces until all arguments were heard and weighed. "Tradition," he said, "gives us the conceptions of right in general; of justice, of truth . . . That it is right to be beneficent, just, true . . . is a matter of *immediate personal* experience." Ward replied: "Had an unlucky *intuitionist* made such a statement as this, when would he have heard the last of it?" *The Nineteenth Century*, March, 1878, p. 534.

[70] *Ibid.*

[71] *Ibid.*

[72] "Professor Clifford on the Sin of Credulity," *Spectator*, 1877, reprinted in *Aspects of Religious and Scientific Thought*, (London, 1899), pp. 55-56.

[73] "The Wish to Believe," *The Nineteenth Century*, Feb., 1882 and Sept., 1883.

[74] These figures may well be Fitzjames Stephen and Wilfred Ward's father, W. G. Ward. The two men often debated these issues at the meetings of the Metaphysical Society.

[75] *Op. cit.*, Feb., 1882, p. 210.

[76] *Ibid.*, Sept., 1883, p. 460.

[77] *Ibid.*

[78] Ibid., p. 461.

[79] "Wilfred Ward's 'Wish to Believe', in *Comtemporary Thought and Thinkers*, I, 1894, 367.

[80] J. H. Newman, *Sermons, Chiefly on the Theory of Religious Belief*, 1843, p. 223.

[81] Matthew Arnold, "A Psychological Parallel," *The Contemporary Review*, 28 (1876), 908.

[82] *Last Essays on Church and Religion*, 1903, p. 27.

[83] *Literature and Dogma*, Ungar ed., 1970, pp. 38-39.

[84] T. H. Green, *Faith and the Witness of God*, 1883, p. 88.

[85] *Ibid.*, p. 98.

[86] J. S. Mill, "Theism," *Collected Works*, X, 1969, 483, 485.

[87] William James, *The Will to Believe and Other Essays*, 1897, p. 14.

# III

The debate over the ethics of religious belief in the 1870's and beyond was many-faceted. Considerable publicity was given to the issue of clerical subscription and to the general philosophical debate. But there were other moral questions that were of great urgency. One was the moral consideration of the utility of a religious conformity which was not wholly candid. Another was the matter of withholding one's disbelief or encouraging beliefs in others which oneself rejected. This was often the dilemma of an agnostic husband or father. Even the no-nonsense James Fitzjames Stephen continued to piously escort his wife and children to church long after he had given up the church's belief. While he took pains to instruct his children in the reasons for his rational religious belief, when doubt took over Stephen appears not to have bothered to instruct them in his new found reasons for not believing. John Morley recommended that a sceptic inform his children of his unbelief but advised that such knowledge should be kept from one's parents.

To a people raised on Benthamite utilitarianism and Butler's probabilism, it is not surprising that the question of the utility of religion should play an especially large role in discussions of religious conformity in a period of unsettlement and doubt. J. S. Mill had clearly given a large place to such pragmatic considerations in his valedictory essays on religion. In "The Utility of Religion" Mill had said that, in view of agnosticism,

> it is not enough to aver . . . that there can never be any conflict between truth and utility; that if religion be false, nothing but good can be the consequence of rejecting it . . . (For) when the only truth ascertainable is that nothing can be known, we do not, by this knowledge, gain any new fact by which to guide ourselves; we are, at best, only disabused of our trust in some former guide-mark which, though itself fallacious, may have pointed in the same direction with the best indications we have, and if it happens to be more conspicuous and legible, may have kept us right when they might have been overlooked. It is, in short, perfectly conceivable that religion may be morally useful without being intellectually sustainable.[1]

There was a surprisingly widespread belief among Victorian intellectuals, including freethinkers, that with the demise of Christian doctrine there would be a serious crisis and decline in public morals. In a symposium in the first issue (1877) of *The Nineteenth Century* the question of "The Influence Upon Morality of a Decline in Religious Belief" was debated by a dozen eminent writers, including Fitzjames Stephen, Huxley, Clifford, Frederic Harrison, Dean Church, R. H. Hutton, and W. G. Ward. Clifford was the only contributor who did not predict moral decline. Curiously, this is not far from equating unbelief and sin, a notion under heavy attack at the time and on its way out. But if virtues such as charity, brotherly love, hope, and self-sacrifice were to dissolve with the loss of the theological substructure, then might it not be wise to conform to such a foundation, though it be intellectually unsustainable? The educated class had a special responsibility not to disturb the foundations of the social structure, or so many argued, for considering the delicacy of the social fabric, scrupulous concern for personal hypocrisy in conforming religiously was certainly morbid and egoistic. Louis Greg put the issue: "The main question then, that the agnostic has to face is, which course of action will tend most to the good or advancement of humanity, going to church, or absenting himself therefrom."[2] If the unbeliever is forced to acknowledge that from the life of the Church, its worship, moral admonitions, and service far more good than harm derives, then he must not scruple because he cannot accept all the teaching. Would we, for instance, withhold our child from a school because not all its subjects were well taught? Greg summed up the matter:

> It has been laid down . . . that a man has no right to set others an example which shall induce them to listen to teachings which he considers in part at least, erroneous. No! not if he can give and they can receive something more true; but this being impossible, as undoubtedly it is, let him assist and advise them to attend where he must allow they will gain some good.[3]

The supposition here is, of course, that something better, a more engaging and truer foundation was not forthcoming. While few agnostics and no positivist could agree with such a judgment, most of the educated class did. Henry Sidgwick defended a latitudinarianism and reserve *for laymen*, despite the danger of promoting an attitude of thinking lightly of conscious inconsistency and insincerity, on just such grounds of moral utility.

> The service which religion undeniably renders to society lies primarily in its influence on the moral and social feelings, and that Multitudism tends to keep this influence alive in many cases in which a strict doctrinalism would tend to destroy it. If a man severs himself from the worship of his parents . . . he will, in many cases, form no new religious ties . . . and in consequence the influence of religion on his life will be liable to be impaired, and with it the influence of that higher morality which Christianity . . . powerfully supports and inspires; so that his life will in consequence be liable to become more selfish, frivolous, and worldly, even if he does not lapse into recognized immorality.[3]

Fitzjames Stephen could not finally accept Greg's advice but did not doubt the loss which would accompany unbelief; nor did he see anything which might replace it. While we cannot easily judge the effects of unbelief in a nation of believers, "if we should ever," says Stephen, "see a generation of men, especially a generation of Englishmen, to whom the word 'God' has no meaning at all, we should get a light on the subject which might be lurid enough."[4]

Yet, come what may, Stephen was compelled to hold that theology and morality stand to each other in the same relation as facts and legislation. "No one would propose to support by artificial means a law passed under a mistake, for fear it should have to be altered. To say that the truth of a theological doctrine must not be questioned, lest the discovery of its falsehood should produce a bad moral effect, is in principle precisely the same thing."[5]

According to Stephen, the support   which a creed gives to a system of morals is irrelevant to the question of that creed's truth. On the other hand, the goodness of a system of morals cannot be determined until "the question whether the theology on which it rests is true or false . . . If it is founded on a false theology, it is founded on a false estimate of the consequences of human actions; and so far as that is the case, it cannot be good."[6]

Huxley, on the other hand, believed that morality would hold its own without theological supports. But even if he were wrong and without this or that dogma the human race would "lapse into bipedal cattle, more brutal than the beasts," Huxley's next question would still be "to ask for the proof of the truth of the dogma."[7] If the proof is forthcoming all well and good, but if not, "then I verily believe the human race will go its evil way." Huxley took great consolation in the reflection that, however bad posterity may become, "so long as they hold by the plain rule of not pretending to believe what they have no reason to believe, because it may be to their advantage so to pretend, they will not have reached the lowest depths of immorality."[8]

The utilitarian argument for a sceptical acquiescence and conformity to the teachings of the church did, however, find support among the most candid and respected philosophers in England. We have indicated the position taken by Mill at the end of his life. T. H. Green made a similar plea in his moving and affecting sermon on *Faith*, preached to students and senior members of Balliol College in 1878. While doctrinal tests may disqualify a man from ministerial functions, Green believed no such barrier stood in the way of the layman. Without participation in the society of the church the spiritual aspirations symbolized and made present in its worship and life would likely be lost. "It is often for want of this cooperation," writes Green, "that faith, as a spiritual principle, tends to languish in those to whom the traditional dogmatic expression of it has become impossible. Such persons are much too ready to acquiesce in isolation as a necessary result of their opinions." It is surely a weakness, Green reproves, "when we are not pressed for our opinions to make much of them . . . as to be excluded or exclude ourselves from joining in a common activity, the spirit of which we inwardly reverence and would gladly make our own, while in separation we are almost certain to lose it."[9]

Green's student and younger colleague, Bernard Bosanquet gave as little place to dogmatic opinions and alleged facts as did Green, but extended his warrant for conformity, despite doctrinal scepticism, to the clergy. The central matter, in his view, was whether the causes to which the church is committed are worth promoting, and whether one is suited for such a life work. "But to anyone who has been able to decide (this) main question in the affirmative, the question of veracity would be so greatly modified as to present little difficulty."[10]

The growing acquiescence in this kind of utilitarian argument for conformity and reserve was blunted by the appearance of John Morley's *On Compromise*. It was hailed by many churchmen as a kind of secular "rod of God's anger" against the indifferentists in the church. Morley was profoundly distressed by what he saw becoming "an inveterate national characteristic," viz., a profound distrust of principles and "the paramount wisdom of counting the narrow, immediate and personal expediency for everything."[11] He was especially provoked to see his master, J. S. Mill, give support to this pernicious sentiment. The chapter in *On Compromise* entitled "Of the Possible Utility of Error" was directed specifically against Mill's proposition that a belief may be "morally useful without being intellectually sustainable." By such speech Mill was justifying "all those conformities, compliances, economies, and accommodations, that men are naturally ready to practice"[12] to avoid the discomforts of dissent or of shaking the foundations of the spiritual shelter of the masses.

Morley took it upon himself to systematically answer the numerous arguments proffered for countenancing religious error on pragmatic grounds. It was said, for example, that a false opinion may be clothed with good associations, especially moral virtues. The answer, Morley counters, is that "in making false notions the proofs or close associates of true ones, you are exposing the latter to the ruin which awaits the former."[13] Virtues such as honesty or industry, which are associated with the fear of hell, may well dissolve with loss of that belief. To the argument that the minds of the masses are not open or ready for speculative reasons, Morley answers that superstition itself is the main cause of this failure. Moreover, as Condorcet and Clifford argued, erroneous beliefs tend to foster other erroneous ways of thinking. Likewise, those many who argue that a false opinion may be less hurtful than its premature demolition are wrong. Why? Because they fail to realize that without the removal of a bad element it "otherwise tends to propagate itself . . . or tends at the best to make the surrounding mass of error more inveterate."[14] One must look not only to the expediency of the present hour but to the future well-being of society.

To the argument of a Bosanquet or Walter Pater, in his review of *Robert Elsmere*,[15] viz., that a man should not scruple over lack of candor in doctrinal conformity when he has an opportunity of exerting a useful influence on the public, Morley asks; "What influence can a man exert, that is more useful than that of a protester against what he counts false opinions in the most decisive and important of all regions of thought? What better service can a man do than to furnish the world with an example of faithful dealing with his own conscience and with his fellows?"[16]

Morley seems to have been listened to. At least the principles he preached had an effect on the clergy in the eighteen seventies and eighties. Most clergymen, for example, thought Stopford Brooke was right to leave the Church in 1880 because of his disbelief in the miracles of the creeds.

The secession of a clergyman from the established Church was often a painful and bitter experience — a rending asunder of bones and marrow. The cost to the man, his family and the community was often very high. The anguish felt all around in such a move was portrayed with skill and compassion in Mrs. Humphrey Ward's story of *Robert Elsmere*. After hearing Elsmere's account of his doubts, his old tutor, T. H. Green, reminded him "that there are many men. . . . who hold very much what I imagine your opinions now are, or will settle into, who are still in the Church of England, doing admirable work there!" But Elsmere "cannot conceive it," for he cannot "preach another Easter Day sermon to a congregation that have both a moral and a legal right to demand from (him) an implicit belief in the material miracle!"[17]

Elsmere's action was what was generally expected of a clergyman who did not believe in the central miracles of the faith. Mrs. Ward's view of what constituted the proper response to unsettlement was the most common one as late as 1890. But that was to change, and a decade into the new century Mrs. Ward would have Elsmere stay. She told why in a drama of a modernist clergyman entitled *The Case of Richard Meynell*. The profound influence of historical and philosophical criticism, she wrote, demanded that in the last years of the century clergy not secede to something without, but join in the task of *reconstruction* from within. The argument from utility still had force, but from the eighties on, the foremost arguments for staying in the church had to do with the right and duty of reinterpretation. This involved the momentous question of the legitimacy and limits of a symbolical or metaphorical interpretation of the Bible and the doctrines of the creed.

The new situation is portrayed by F. Warre Cornish, with less narrative skill but with a depth of understanding equal to Mrs. Ward's, in his novel *Sunningwell* (1899). It is the story of the difficulties of Canon More, a sensitive, devout, liberal clergyman, serving a Cathedral chapter in the 1870's. Cornish portrays the liberal priest's dilemma faced with symbolic interpretation. When gently accused by a member of his own chapter of maintaining an unhelpful reserve in his treatment of the miracles, Canon More can only reply that "If we do, it is perhaps because we see, more clearly than you do, the difficulty of the problem. It is easy to drive us into a corner, with the 'false' or 'true' dilemma." The better way in such times, More argues, is reserve and patience. But what, asks his fellow Canon, are we to *say* about such doctrines as the Incarnation and Resurrection? More replies that while he finds it impossible to accept simply and without comment, as if there were no difficulty in it, the literal, material account, as told in the Gospels, on the other hand, if he were "to say I do not believe in the Resurrection, he should be saying what is untrue." Nevertheless, he cannot precisely explain it. But if words have no clear meaning shouldn't the creeds be given up? More gives two reasons why they should be retained. "If we tried to mend the language . . . we should harden the differences." New formulas bind, while old formulas gain latitude. Secondly, while the thought expressed in the creed is not today *identical* with that of the past, it has an analogous meaning. " 'Descended into hell' may not represent to me as simple a fact as 'was buried' but I can find a true meaning in the words, though very likely not the same as the original meaning." Some accommodation of the formulas to a non-natural sense, More insists, is practiced by all, and who is to limit the degree or extent?

Canon More was compelled to speak out while preferring silence. He also felt a duty to stay in the church, although he felt compelled to give up his living. His position was similar to Rowland Williams'. He likened it to "standing in the doorway, as it were, to prevent the door being closed in the face of questions which call for answer, not exclusion; and that to go out would be betraying a trust."[18]

The call to stay in the church and defend a symbolic interpretation of the formularies was heard with considerably more frequency in the nineties. The work of men like Arnold and Green had had their effect. However, the man who, through his own sincerity and pastoral concern, encouraged others to speak out was Edwin Abbott, biblical scholar and Headmaster of the City of London School. In 1886 he published *The Kernel and the Husk: Letters on Spiritual Christianity*. The book was dedicated to "the doubters of this generation" who, wishing to join in Christian worship, held back or felt dishonesty in doing so because they assumed that their faith must rest on belief in the biblical miracles. Abbott wished to "give young men a religion that would wear" and by this he meant one freed from belief in miracle. In the concluding letters of the book he addressed the problem whether a man can remain a minister of the Church of England and be a believer in non-miraculous Christianity. The Clerical Subscription Act's "general assent" protected such a man legally, but the lack of candor between the minister and his people remained. The difficulty might well be removed by publicity, but this assumes that a metaphorical interpretation was possible and permissible—an assumption without support in 1886. The dilemma for Abbott, as for Canon More, and those of like mind, was fear of giving their congregations a false impression of their belief and yet an aversion to using the pulpit of the National Church as a platform for attacking the received-view of the creeds.

Abbott believed the time had come for forthright admission of the liberal position. Only such bold action would bring a clear condemnation or authorization of non-natural interpretation. However, the priest's admission must not be made in public worship but to the bishop, for his determination. Attacks from the pulpit on the old forms of belief, Abbott was convinced, are bound to be construed into attacks upon the spirit. His advice was: "Do not attack their material belief; preach your spiritual belief." In this way you teach a truth "without sacrificing your own convictions; and at the same time insensibly prepare the younger portion of your flock to detach the material part of their faith from the spiritual."[19]

Abbott's proposal was attractive. It allowed for candor and positive action for change, yet counselled moderation and a slow process of innovation. However, the book was attacked by Charles Gore—a fact which gave Abbott's proposal a wider audience. It also launched Gore on a more than quarter-century struggle against non-natural interpretations of the creeds. The claim that men should exercise the church's sacred ministry while openly rejecting the natural sense of the creeds required, in Gore's words, "a protest so clear, so broad, so firm, that the verdict of the church's conscience shall be quite unmistakable."[20]

Thus began a new and often pathetic chapter in the debate over the ethics of belief. The pathos lay in the renewal of charges and counter charges of dishonesty. Both parties claimed their opponents put respect for truth in the second place, hallowed, covert loyalties first. Both sides cited Morley on the inroads of "disastrous compromise." Gore led the attack on the modernists and, it must be said, because of his failure to perceive what was, for the liberals, *the* central issue, caused a good deal of mischief for years to come.

Gore's position is instructive. He expresses unambiguously what, for lack of a better term, might be called the "neo-traditionalist" position. He also reveals that position's Achilles heel. Gore, and those who joined him in the volume of essays entitled *Lux Mundi*, claimed allegiance to the two loyalties of the Victorian moral conscience: a thorough-going intellectual openness and a forthright assent to the creedal standards of the church. This is evident in Gore's Preface to *Lux Mundi*, where he affirms that the essayists wrote "as servants of the Catholic Creed and Church," yet in the conviction that the intellectual transformations of the day would "necessitate some general restatement of (theology's) claim and meaning." Gore could boldly say "that it is impossible in any way to withdraw the historical basis of Christianity from the freest and frankest criticism." Persons who say "Let the Old Testament be frankly criticized ... but not the New Testament ... must be utterly repudiated ... (for) the Creed has no other line of defense behind the New Testament documents." One cannot "pretend that the validity of our Creeds is independent of the issue of such criticism."[21]

On the other hand, recognizing that criticism had brought to light the "idealizing element in the Old Testament," i.e., myth and legend, Gore could yet argue on theological prepossession, not critical results, that "the reason of course is obvious enough why what can be admitted in the Old Testament, could not without results disastrous to the Christian Creed, be admitted in the New."[22] Gore, the courageous defender of criticism, assumed and thus prescribed the results in the case of New Testament research. He was so convinced of the historical trustworthiness of the New Testament that he could only impute evil motives to those who arrived at negative conclusions on points which might affect adversely the historic interpretation of the Creeds. Gore simply assumed the historical intention of the apostolic writers. "Their intentions," he could write as late as 1921, "were conspicuously honest and simple. They appear to have no design except to record things as they happened."[23]

Gore was correct, as was Newman, in insisting on the role of temper of mind in the assessment of evidence. He continuously stressed the fact that "what seems to us proven or not proven, probable or improbable — will depend on what our *praejudicia* are, i.e., our preconceptions, intuitions, experiences, sentiments, feelings."[24] But, as we shall see, this epistemological premise allowed Gore to peremptorily dismiss what he considered "destructive criticism" because such critics "reach the results they reach, not from considerations properly historical, but because their mind is occupied with a certain view of the world which indisposes them to the conclusions of the Creed."[25]

Gore, and men like R. C. Moberly and Scott Holland, had given up the Tractarian view of biblical inspiration defended by Pusey and J. B. Mozley. They retrenched to a new line of defense: the historicity of the miraculous events rehearsed in the creeds. Men who could not confess belief in the literal events of Christ's birth and resurrection were, to Gore's mind, predisposed not to accept the world of Christian supernaturalism, and could not with sincerity hold ministerial office in the church. Honesty of profession and loyalty to the faith must be hedged in by certain essentials. Essentials, however, whose historical warrant was, as Gore himself insisted, to be adjudicated by "the freest and frankest criticism." But the old question remained. If the creeds are the *terminus a quo* of theological work then was not Frederick Temple right that the conclusions of "criticism" were prescribed and the study precluded?

The Liberal critics were attacked not only by the likes of Gore but by freethinking agnostics as well. By the nineties the freethinkers had given considerable ground to the liberal churchmen on matters of biblical criticism. But there were limits. By 1895 Henry Sidgwick had come to believe that laymen could consider their pledge of belief in the Apostles Creed to be relaxed by a common understanding. The case of the clergy was, he thought, otherwise. Liberals who thus sought to open the ranks of the ministry to men who do not believe, say, in the Virgin Birth must "find an inexorable barrier" to veracity and good faith in the necessity of declaring their personal belief in those very doctrines stated in the creed. Sidgwick believed that there was, in the case of the clergy, no common understanding that this pledge was relaxed. He insisted that those who wished to work for a removal of the miraculous element of the Gospel history from Christianity, must work "outside the pale of the Anglican ministry" or be charged with building their modernist edifice "with the untempered mortar of falsehood and evasion of solemn obligations."[26] Sidgwick joined Gore in drawing the line at the common (historical) sense of the creeds.

Sidgwick's essay was answered by one of the younger leaders of the modernist cause, Hastings Rashdall. He asked Sidgwick the obvious question: "why do you draw the line at exactly this point?" Rashdall couldn't understand "why a clergyman should be considered dishonest who does not believe in some particular Gospel miracle if it is admitted that he is not dishonest for not believing that Jonah was swallowed by a whale," unless, of course, "it is urged that in *practice* there is an understanding about the Old Testament which does not exist about the New." In that case, Rashdall insists, "the question is one of what we may call general ethical or spiritual expediency, not of technical veracity."[27]

As to Sidgwick's crucial test, i.e., belief in the miraculous birth of Christ, Rashdall points out that it after all is a matter of critical judgment concerning the evidence. Many able and devout minds consider the evidence weak or even nugatory—cause, at least, for suspended judgment. However wrong such criticism may prove to be, it is honest and "it is impossible to believe that the church will permanently exclude from its ministry those who differ from the majority . . . when it has admitted the principles of free criticism, of accepting or rejecting miraculous narratives on critical grounds."[28]

Rashdall concedes to Sidgwick that, while the decision for the veracious man as to what constitutes essentiality of belief is his own, nevertheless "he must have regard to the actual state of public opinion on the subject."[29] Not that he must be satisfied that common opinion explicitly acknowledges the non-essentiality of the particular belief he wishes to deny or interpret in an uncommon sense. Rather, that he "ought to satisfy himself that this disbelief has already been recognized as falling within the permissible limits . . . as not inconsistent with the formal pledges of a clergyman."[30] If a man can do that he is free of any taint of unveracity. It is then up to the church to decide for or against him.

Rashdall believed that if a man could not clearly discern whether his position does or does not exceed the limits of liberty, "he may surely feel justified in throwing the responsibility upon . . . the Bishop." Rashdall agreed with Abbott that to make such an open avowal to the Bishop "of the sense in which he interprets his pledge" discharges his moral duty. The "clergyman should never in his sermon say what he does not believe," and the extent to which he is bound to proclaim the *whole* of his beliefs depends on expediency, on the circumstances of time and place. Generally the clergy addresses mixed congregations and in such cases "there must be limits to plain speaking—not indeed to *bona fide* private inquiries, but before mixed audiences."[31]

Sidgwick was unconvinced by Rashdall's argument. While the widest latitude of interpretation must be allowed, nevertheless, "the common understanding of language, changing with changes in knowledge and habitual sentiment, must be the test."[32] However difficult it may be in specific cases to decide when exactly a divergence from the literal sense becomes evasive and indefensible, it is easy, Sidgwick contends "to say that some divergences are quite beyond any defensible line." Such, in his view, is the case with the affirmation defended by Rashdall. "The assertion that Jesus Christ was born of a virgin has a perfectly simple and definite negative meaning . . . it is impossible to conceive . . . any admissible qualification by which the phrase could be adapted to the thought of a man who believes that Jesus was the son of Joseph"[33] Rashdall had argued for retention of "conceived by the Holy Ghost of the Virgin Mary" on the grounds that the historical import or spiritual truth of the alleged miracle had to do with belief in Christ's sinlessness — a doctrine held even among Unitarians. But Sidgwick finds it "difficult to treat the suggestion seriously." "There is surely not the slightest chance," he insists, "that any part of any congregation would — without an express declaration that it was the speaker's meaning — understand the affirmation of the miraculous birth to mean an affirmation of the infant's sinlessness."[34]

Sidgwick rejects the view of Abbott and Rashdall that open avowal to the bishop fulfills one's moral obligation. In fact such a private explanation makes the bishop an accomplice in deception.

> Further, I cannot consider that a false statement in the recital of a creed is rendered unobjectionable by a public declaration of its falsity; because it is likely still to give a shock to the moral sentiment of a plain man, who cannot be expected to distinguish clearly between formal and substantial unveracity; moreover, the solemn utterance of untrue words will seem to him a mockery of sacred things and offend his religious sentiment.[35]

Was not Sidgwick here touching a base of feelings widely shared by those educated and common people alike who set a high priority on plain-speaking? On this point the *Lux Mundi* group joined forces with Leslie Stephen, Morley and Sidgwick against the modernists. Gore would keep men of Rashdall's belief out of the ministry of the Church of England. Sidgwick would leave them in, but such toleration would necessitate, on grounds of the simplest veracity, the removal of the Apostles Creed as a test and from its place in the church's service. As time would reveal, neither of these policies would be approved.

At the end of Victoria's reign it appeared that the mass of men, laity and clergy, held that, while non-natural interpretations of most of the Anglican formularies and the "damnatory clauses" of the Athanasian Creed, were permissible, no margin of divergence was allowed the clergy when it came to the historical clauses of the Creeds. The candidate for ordination must give an *ex animo* assent to these articles in their obvious literal sense.

This conclusion was an unstable one, and it was soon shown why. First of all, it became evident that the difficulties with regard to the literal reading of the creeds (Sidgwick's test of a common use of language) was not limited to a few academics full of German criticism. It was felt by a widening circle of ordinary churchmen. But more importantly, the claims being made for the articles of the creeds were, finally, warranted by appeal to the New Testament witness — whose authenticity and meaning were open to historical-critical test. Unless, that is, there were some reasons why such criticism was precluded. The issue left unsettled at the end of the century was whether the scholarly clergyman had a right and duty to carry on his inquiries unhampered by non-scientific restrictions. To trace the resolution of this issue involves pursuing the story into the present century. We must, then, consider one further chapter in the debate and its ambiguous conclusion.[36]

[1] J. S. Mill, *Collected Works*, X, (London, 1969), 405.

[2] "The Agnostic at Church," *The Nineteenth Century* (Jan., 1882), p. 74.

[3] *Ibid.*, p. 75.

[3a] Henry Sidgwick, "The Ethics of Religious Conformity," *International Journal of Ethics* (1896), p. 283.

[4] James Fitzjames Stephen, *Liberty, Equality, Fraternity*, (1873, 2nd ed.), p. 326.

[5] "The Influence Upon Morality of a Decline in Religious Belief," *The Nineteenth Century*, I, (1877), 332.

[6] *Ibid.*, p. 333.

[7] *Ibid.*, p. 539.

[8] Ibid.

[9] T. H. Green, *Witness of God and Faith* (London, 1883), p. 101-02.

[10] Bernard Bosanquet, *International Journal of Ethics*, 8 (1897-98), 392-93.

[11] John Morley, *On Compromise* (London, 1874), pp. 4-5.

[12] John Morley, "Mr. Mill's Three Essays on Religion," *The Fortnightly Review*, 17, N.S., (1875), 113.

[13] *On Compromise*, p. 49.

[14] *Ibid.*, p. 55.

[15] *Essays from The Guardian*, (London, 1910), p. 53f.

[16] *On Compromise*.

[17] Mrs. Humphry Ward, *Robert Elsmere*, II, *The Writings of Mrs. Humphry Ward*, (London, 1911), p. 106-07.

[18] F. Warre Cornish, *Sunningwell* (London, 1899), pp. 256-58, 261, 263.

[19] Edwin Abbott, *The Kernel and the Husk*, (London, 1886), p. 363-64.

[20] Charles Gore, *The Clergy and the Creeds* (London, 1887), pp. 8-9

[21] *The Permanent Creed* (London, 1905), p. 12, 14.

[22] Charles Gore, "The Holy Spirit and Inspiration," *Lux Mundi* (London, 1890), p. 354.

[23] Charles Gore, *Belief in God* (London, 1922) p. 215.

[24] Charles Gore, *Papers Read Before the Synthetic Society*. Unpublished. Bodleian Library. p. 65.

[25] *The Permanent Creed*, p. 16.

[26] *The Ethics of Religious Conformity* (1896) pp. 288-90.

[27] Hastings Rashdall, "Professor Sidgwick on the Ethics of Religious Conformity: A Reply," *International Journal of Ethics*, (Jan., 1897), p. 148.

[28] *Ibid.*, p. 149.

[29] *Ibid.*, p. 157.

[30] *Ibid.*, p. 158.

[31] *Ibid.*, p. 161-63.

[32] Henry Sidgwick, "On Clerical Veracity," *Practical Ethics*, (London, 1898), p. 168.

[33] *Ibid.*, p. 170.

[34] *Ibid.*

[35] *Ibid.*, p. 171.

[36] The story of the debate over the ethics of subscription, the creeds and criticism in the first two decades of this century has been told and the details cannot be reviewed here. Our interest is in the positions taken and their implications. For accounts of the controversy see G. K. A. Bell, *Randall Davidson*; A. Ramsey, *From Gore to Temple*.

# IV

By the turn of the century influential clergymen in the Church of England, such as Hastings Rashdall, Dean Fremantle, and Hensley Henson, were writing critically about the Virgin Birth and the Resurrection narratives. Resolutions were soon pressed to declare against such views. The new Archbishop of Canterbury, Randall Davidson, resisted these efforts for, as he observed, such a declaration "means virtually an addition to our formularies." J. Armitage Robinson, Dean of Westminster, published a statement, at the suggestion of Davidson, which helped dampen the zeal for declaration. Robinson wrote that to insist on the historical fact of the Virgin Birth as a cardinal doctrine of the church "is to confuse the Incarnation with the special mode of the Incarnation." "It is," he asserted, "the act of reassertion by authority of that which is questioned by criticism."[1] The crisis passed for a time, only to reemerge with a greater virulence in the years just before World War I.

In 1911 J. M. Thompson, Dean of Divinity of Magdelen College, Oxford, published *The Miracles of the New Testament*, in which he frankly rejected the miracles of the Virgin Birth and the physical Resurrection. The book caused an outcry and Thompson's license to teach was removed by the Bishop of Winchester, and Gore, now Bishop of Oxford, refused him permission to officiate in his diocese. Thompson was deeply concerned over what he felt was a new and dangerous lack of respect for truth in the church. "We need to remind ourselves," he said, "very seriously of our responsibility for our beliefs," and concluded by commending to his readers the words of W. K. Clifford: "It is wrong in all cases to believe on insufficient evidence; and where it is presumption to doubt and to investigate, there it is worse than presumption to believe."[2]

The following year Canon Hensley Henson published *The Creed in the Pulpit*. He found Thompson's language "gravely inadequate"; its inadequacy was not, however, the issue at stake. The larger question was: "Has Mr. Thompson exceeded the limits of tolerable liberty by publishing the conclusions to which a candid and careful study of Scripture has led him, and which he himself believes to be consistent with an honest acceptance of the Creed?"[3] The Anglican clergyman is pledged at his ordination to a devoted study of the Holy Scriptures, but the issue for Henson was "whether he will fulfill his pledge as a modern student, using the full resources of modern knowledge and the exact methods of modern critical science, or whether he will resolutely ignore both, and limit himself, after the manner of a medieval monk, to the pious task of accumulating patristic comments on the sacred text . . ."[4]

One thing, to Henson's mind, was unquestionable. "In setting a ring-fence about the narratives of Christ's birth and resurrection, and exempting them from the operation of critical methods, allowed to control the rest of the New Testament, Mr. Thompson's opponents have taken up a position which is really impossible to justify."[5]

For years Gore had sought a declaration against those denying the Virgin Birth and the physical Resurrection. The events of 1911-12 finally provoked him to issue a public charge in an Open Letter to his clergy, entitled *The Basis of Anglican Fellowship* (1914). Gore made two points that caused special offense and incited a renewed pamphlet war. First of all, he claimed that recitation of the creeds requires "a personal expression of belief in the occurrence of certain events in history, and these in part strictly miraculous events."[6] Having skirted the question of critical results, Gore went on to insist that it is inconsistent "with the sincerity which ought to attach . . . to public office in the Christian Church, that a man should pledge himself to the constant recitation of these Creeds . . . if he personally does not believe that these miraculous events occurred."[7]

Gore wished that another Pascal might rise up to smite the modernists who, like the Jesuits, were "led on in a special atmosphere to adopt a position and maintain a claim which, looked at in the light of common morality, proves utterly unjustifiable."[8] Thus Gore not only fenced the clerical scholar's critical freedom but impugned his moral integrity.

Among those who replied to Gore's Open Letter were four of the outstanding historical theologians of the period. H. M. Gwatkin, Dixie Professor of Ecclesiastical History in Cambridge, was an Evangelical and unsympathetic toward the modernist theology. He could not imagine the doctrines of the creeds disproved. Yet he denounced Gore's attack on criticism. "Sound criticism," he wrote, "is as truly a divine revelation as Scripture itself, and we shall fail in our duty to truth and to Him who was the truth if we foreclose the question . . .. the question is one of evidence."[9] The only defense against a false criticism is better criticism. "You, my Lord, are a scholar," Gwatkin reminded Gore, "and you will understand me if I remind you that scholarship will always correct the errors of scholarship — provided only we do not call in authority to cut the knot . . . We need only a little of the patience and trust in truth which is so conspicuously wanting in an appeal to authority."[10]

Gwatkin's Cambridge colleague J. F. Bethune-Baker made a similar plea for the right of clergymen to study freely the foundations of the Christian faith and publish their results. He pointed out that as to the alleged facts, "the sanction of the church of all ages is simply the sanction of the church of the second century." Until recently the church was not in a position to critically examine and revise the version of the facts given by the early church. But today that is no longer true and students "are better able to estimate the historical worth of particular narratives in our Gospels than was the church of the first or any succeeding century."[11]

Bethune-Baker suggested an interpretation of the Virgin Birth and the physical restoration of Christ which gained wide acceptance among modernist churchmen and is commonplace today in liberal theology. He argued that, unlike the Incarnation and the Resurrection, the Virgin Birth and bodily restoration of Christ were not attested to by the religious experience of the church. They are not theological or spiritual facts but rather "early intellectual inferences drawn by some of the first disciples from the genuinely religious experience which they enjoyed of the personal power and influence of Jesus in His lifetime and His presence with them after His death on the Cross."[12]

According to Bethune-Baker, the Apostles' Creed is not "a string of historical statements" but rather "a religious valuation of the facts" of the faith, such as the Incarnation and Resurrection. Thus a clergyman who believes in the latter doctrines "is entitled to recite the whole of the Apostles' Creed as his profession of faith without being exposed to any breach of the moral principle of sincerity of profession."[13] Such a clergyman is, more correctly, not "entitled" but *morally obligated* to recite phrases such as "born of the Virgin Mary," for, as Bethune-Baker argued, they "are the only words in the Creed which express the doctrine." The terms "may not be the terms we would choose, but they are the only terms in which the society of which he is a member . . . expresses the belief which he himself holds in common with them."[14] Sidgwick would no doubt have thought this interpretation disingenuous in the extreme, but it was a position that was to gain wide favor. The modernists could argue that it was thereby justified to claim for itself, in time, the test of common usage demanded by Sidgwick.

Two of the most incisive replies to Bishop Gore's challenge came from his own diocese of Oxford. They are interesting not primarily as replies to Gore but rather as pointing up the problematic nature of the position he represented. B. H. Streeter, editor of *Foundations*, commended Gore for calling attention to the moral issue of clerical veracity but was, nevertheless, compelled to dissent from his general conclusions.

In his Open Letter Gore had acknowledged that the "damnatory clauses" of the Athanasian Creed had long been recited, and properly so, with "a mental reservation which it does not really convey." This is justified, Gore urged, because the Athanasian Creed is really only a "canticle." This Streeter regarded as simply untrue, historically and in the present life of the church. The Articles, the Prayer Book and the plain man "all agree in calling it a Creed." Furthermore,

> it is ordered to be used as a *substitute* for the usual Creed; and that, be it observed, not on unimportant occasions, but at the most solemn festivals of the church. Moreover, those who most desire to effect a change and those who most vehemently resist it, are agreed in doing so, because they regard the document as having creedal force.[15]

Streeter pointed out that, on Gore's terms, "those who claimed to treat as 'canticles' some other documents, which the church styles 'creeds,' could at least plead that they were only doing what the Bishop of Oxford and all his brethren have been doing throughout a long and beneficent ministerial career."[16]

Since Gore was concerned with historical warrants and precedent, Streeter calls his attention to the fact that

> in the actual Creed which was sanctioned by the Council of Nicaea, which is popularly regarded as having a certain primacy among the Councils, there is no mention of the Virgin Birth; or of the fact that the only form of Creed, which has ecumenical sanction, begins with the words, 'we believe,' which as the Bishop concedes, implies a less strictly personal form of assent than the western formula, 'I believe'.[17]

The weakest point in the position maintained by Gore, but one shared by hosts of other clerics and churchmen, was the necessity of drawing a distinction between the historical and purely symbolical clauses of the creeds. By common consent, several of the clauses of the Apostles' Creed had long been recognized as symbolical, e.g., those which speak of "descended into Hell" or "sitteth at the right hand of God." Gore conceded as much. But how is one to distinguish which clauses are historical and which symbolic? Gore offered a formula:

> Human language is practically limited by what has fallen within present human experience. With regard, therefore, to what lies outside present human experience, we can only be taught, or formulate our beliefs, in *symbolical* language . . . So it is about the being of God, or about the beginnings and endings of things, or about heaven and hell. When I say Christ ascended into heaven, I am first of all referring to a certain symbolical, but actual and historical demonstration which our Lord gave to His disciples forty days after His resurrection. But when I say 'He descended into Hell,' and also when in a more general sense I say 'He ascended into heaven and sitteth, etc.', I confess to the use of metaphor in an historical statement, because the historical statement carries me outside the world of present possible experience, and symbolical language is the only language that I can use.[18]

Gore considered a clause such as "He ascended into heaven and sitteth at the right hand of God" as a crucial test. He agreed that the latter part of the clause is pure symbolism, but that "He ascended . . ." contains an historical event. "So far as the first part of the clause is concerned it must be understood to refer to an historical incident, viz., that the body of Jesus Christ forty days after his resurrection rose before His disciples' eyes upwards from the earth and vanished."[19]

Numerous critics thought Gore's distinction questionable. Many stories in the Bible have a *prima facie* reference to events supposed to have occurred "within the limits of human experience," e.g., the stories of the Patriarchs, of Jonah or Daniel, but which are no longer regarded as historical.[20] Streeter pointed out that the distinction drawn by Gore "might possibly have been understood by the learned Fathers of Alexandria" but that it was highly improbable that it would have been understood by the early church, "and it has never been recognized by the vast mass of Christians."[21] Nor are so-called phenomenal occurrences such as the Incarnation and Resurrection "historical" in our common understanding of the term. Kierkegaard and Karl Barth would soon make us aware of that! As Streeter observed:

> The exact manner of the union of the Divine and Human in the person of Christ, and the exact nature of the Life beyond the grave, are both . . . conceptions which carry one "outside the world of present experience" . . . Thus the hard and fast distinction which (Gore) makes between the clauses which affirm the Incarnation and Resurrection on the one hand, and those which relate to Creation, Heaven, Hell and Judgment on the other, breaks down.[22]

Among the most important criticisms of Gore, because of the eminence of the writer, was William Sanday's pamphlet, "Bishop Gore's Challenge to Criticism." For Sanday the issue was crucial for it had to do with freedom of criticism and Gore, he feared, was far too peremptory in his conclusions. His "wholesale and over-emphatic references to the conclusiveness of the evidence are not promising to the eye of the scholar. The wish is too evidently the father of the thought."[23] As for Gore's mixed historical-symbolic interpretation of the Ascension, Sanday would contend for a straight-forward symbolical interpretation, as in the case of the heavenly Session. Sanday called as witness Bishop Westcott, who had written that "the change which Christ revealed at the Ascension was not a change of place, but a change of state, not local but spiritual." "I do not think," Sanday concluded, "that the *evidence* is sufficient to convince us that 'the physical elevation' of the Lord's body really happened as an external, objective fact."[24]

The problematic nature of Gore's approach to the creeds was analyzed further by the philosopher A. E. Taylor, in a searching discussion of the relationship between theology and history. "I do not understand," wrote Taylor,

> on what principle the line of delimitation between the two classes of historical *Credenda* is to be drawn . . . I gather that Dr. Gore's own view is that the principle of distinction is itself an historical one—certain *Credenda* have long been understood (but by whom?) to be expressed in symbolic language, others not so, and the line must continue to be drawn always just where it was drawn in the past (in the fourth century?) . . . I cannot help thinking that one would only have to go sufficiently far back in the history of the church to find a time when a Council of Dr. Gore's Episcopal predecessors would either have condemned his 'symbolic' Ascension, or have left it uncondemned only because a distinction so clear to his mind would have been unintelligible to theirs.[25]

Gore often labored the point that he wished to give the fullest liberty to the proposals of the critics — but always with the qualification of his own precise limits. The matter of legitimate limits was the issue. The need for such a determination was obvious, but so, it became apparent, was the problem of specifying any restriction. This was revealed in Bishop Frederic Chase's widely read *The Gospels in the Light of Historical Criticism*. Chase was an able biblical scholar and, while supportive of Gore, was put off by his failure to appreciate the thrust of the criticism of men like Streeter and Sanday.

Chase insisted that it must be said "broadly and emphatically that the primary duty of a man is honestly to seek the truth." This means the scholar "must not set out on his inquiry with his mind already made up as to the result. He must candidly consider all the evidence . . . and follow the guidance of the evidence to whatever conclusions it may lead him."[26] But curiously, Chase adds another hermeneutical principle which, he insists, is incumbent on any "purely scientific worker" as such, *viz.*, "to take account of the Creed of the church." This is so because the "Creed brings before him a human judgment on the largest scale as to the origins of the Christian religion . . . and that interpretation of the life of the Founder, through its belief in which the Church as a matter of history has done its work."[27] This is an odd principle to thrust upon the biblical critic; a putting on its head, certainly, the directive to test the formularies "by the sure warrant of Scripture!"

Chase insisted that the duty of the man is also the duty of the clergyman, "for assuredly his ordination did not alter his essential obligations as a man." Ah, but with this qualification: "the clergyman has also a duty as an accredited teacher in a church which holds the historic faith as expressed in the Apostles Creed."[28] The clergyman has, then, really two loyalties: to truth and to the historic faith of the church. What if a clergyman, through candid investigation, must deny as historical the miraculous accounts of Jesus' birth? He has fulfiled his duty as a man, but is that sufficient? Not, Chase argues, in the case of a clergyman, "because . . . to the sincerity of the student must be added the sincerity of the teacher in a body which holds and proclaims a certain definite belief." The clergyman must decide where his duty lies, but he cannot, to Chase's mind, have it both ways. He must decide "whether he is not sacrificing his intellectual honesty" or "whether he is acting fairly towards the church and towards its members."[29] While a man should not be expected to excommunicate himself if he believes the church's formularies need revision in light of biblical evidence, nevertheless, the church, as any society, must lay down its principles to which its office bearers must conform.

Few clergymen denied Chase's analysis of the dual responsibility of the clergy and the right of the church to control its officers. Nevertheless, to say as much is to state the problem, not to solve it. Hensley Henson perceived this and called for a rejection of the conflicting duties:

> If dissent from the formularies, though legitimate as fashioning the personal beliefs of the preacher, may only be admitted into his public teaching at the risk of his ejection from office, is it not obvious that sincerity of utterance in the pulpit will be discouraged, and a premium placed on an uncandid economy of speech which might too easily become demoralizing? Are the two distinctions which are commonly drawn, on the one hand between withdrawing a teacher's credentials and fettering free inquiry and research, and, on the other hand, between the position of an official and that of a private member of the church, really sound?
>
> If, as the Apostle says, the church is 'the pillar and the ground of truth', then to teach in the church's name must primarily mean to teach the truth sincerely. No doubt on the ancient assumption that the truth may be securely identified with the *chose jugée* of official

decisions, it will follow that any divergence from the officialy prescribed doctrine may be taken to argue a conscious and deliberate departure from the truth, but in a church which recognizes the duty of 'unfettered study' and the liberty of private judgment, it is evident that such an absolute identification between the truth and the church's official determinations is not, and cannot reasonably be, made, and, therefore, that at least the possibility of a sincere teaching of truth otherwise than as officially prescribed is admitted. In every case where this actually happens, to withdraw the teacher's credentials must needs imply on the part of the church a repudiation of its own character and function.[30]

Henson recognized that the church required that securities be taken to protect its life against false and harmful influence, but he saw this as resting principally in "the personal character and the technical knowledge of the teacher" which should be determined prior to ordination. "But," he insisted, "the question of liberty in teaching stands on another footing and belongs to that primary obligation of sincerity which attaches to the Christian profession itself."[31]

Henson's plea to untie the knot of a dual and possibly conflicting responsibility of the clergyman *quo* scholar and licensed teacher in the church, was not widely heeded. The bishops, especially, wished to muddle through, and leave the moral problem in ambiguous suspension. This is evident in the declarations of the Bishops between 1908 and 1922. The pamphlet war of 1914 was followed by the demand by Gore and others that the Bishops in Convocation should make an authoritative declaration on the historic facts of the Creeds. After many petitions and two days of high level debate, the following Resolutions were passed *nem con.*:

"1. We call attention to the resolution which was passed in this House on May 10th, 1905, as follows: —

That this House is resolved to maintain unimpaired the Catholic Faith in the Holy Trinity and the Incarnation as contained in the Apostles' and Nicene Creeds, and in the *Quicunque Vult*, and regards the Faith there presented, both in statements of doctrine and in statement of fact, as the necessary basis on which the teaching of the church reposes.

We further desire to direct attention afresh to the following resolution which was unanimously agreed to by the Bishops of the Anglican Communion attending the Lambeth Conference of 1908: —

The Conference, in view of tendencies widely shown in the writings of the present day, hereby places on record *its conviction that the historical facts stated in the Creeds are an essential part of the Faith of the Church.*

2. These resolutions we desire solemnly to reaffirm, and in accordance therewith we express our deliberate judgment that the *denial* of any of the historical facts stated in the Creeds goes beyond the limits of legitimate interpretation, and gravely imperils that sincerity of profession which is plainly incumbent on the Ministers of Word and Sacrament. At the same time, recognizing that our generation is called to face new problems raised by historical criticism, we are anxious not to lay unnecessary burdens upon consciences, nor unduly to limit freedom of thought and inquiry whether among clergy or laity. We desire, therefore, to lay stress on the need for considerateness in dealing with that which is tentative and provisional in the thought and work of earnest and reverent students.[32]

The Resolution was conciliatory, but obviously ambiguous; one could not deny the historical facticity of the creedal statements but one could be "tentative and provisional," apparently, about what was historical and what was not. A Petition presented by the Council of the Churchman's Union and a number of university professors was more straightforward: "While asserting without reserve our belief in the Incarnation and Resurrection of our Lord Jesus Christ, we submit that a wide liberty of belief should be allowed with regard to the mode and attendant circumstances of both."[33] The statements of the Bishops and the Professors were not compatible, but Archbishop Davidson in his summation of the debate, by attempting to set the two statements out of their immediate contexts, urged that there was no inconsistency between them: "Put the two documents, the Petition and our Resolution side by side, dismissing all thought of who are the men who are supporting either of them and I confess that I find nothing in the two that is radically or essentially inconsistent."[34]

Gore was outraged by Davidson's seemingly uncandid attempt at compromise. He wrote Davidson:

> I understood that we had agreed upon a form of words which substantially said no to a specific claim of Rashdall and his friends: viz., that a man might (deliberately and finally) deny that our Lord was born of a virgin or that he rose again from the grave in his body, and still remain an acting clergyman, reciting the Creeds . . . I cannot therefore accept as fair your statement (as I understood it) that we are not by our declaration rejecting the petition of the Liberal Council *if we have regard to its known meaning* . . . If we have not done this we have done nothing . . . Of course you can say 'we have not, *as far as their words go*, rejected their petition?' But that I think is quite unreal. Precisely what we have done is to say no to their petition as it is meant. If we are not understood to have done this, the whole weary matter will begin again.[35]

Davidson wrote to Gore apologizing for his clumsy speech and reaffirming "that we ought in present circumstances formally to declare that a man who denies 'any of the historical facts stated in the Creeds' is, if he continues to minister, violating the conditions which are incumbent upon such a ministry."[36] Gore was satisfied by this reassurance, and the modernists, apparently, were pacified by Davidson's speech.

The modernists were, in fact, victorious, as the years following were to make plain. All talk of "denial of any of the historical facts stated in the Creeds" was soon left behind. The forms shifted to the affirmation of belief in the *doctrine* of the Incarnation and away from the mode of its representation in Scripture and tradition. For example, in 1922 the Upper House of Convocation declared "its conviction that adhesion to the teachings of the Catholic Church as set forth in the 'Nicene' Creed—and in particular concerning the eternal preexistence of the Son of God, His true Godhead, and His Incarnation—is essential to the life of the Church, and calls attention to the fact that the Church commissions as its ministers those only who have solemnly expressed such adhesion."[37]

By 1920 it had become widely recognized that the ethical issues of subscription were dependent on the results of theological scholarship. This was well put by A. E. J. Rawlinson in an essay on "Clerical Veracity," written in 1915:

What is desirable, in short, is that the ethical question should be dropped as an uncharitable irrelevance, and the ecclesiastical question shelved on the ground that it is inexpedient at the present time to press it, until the theological question, which is the really important issue, has been faced and considered upon its merits, and until a more general agreement has been reached with regard to it than can be said to exist among Christian scholars and thinkers at the moment.[38]

This was wise advice—if accompanied by an appeal for the relaxing or abolition of subscription. Such, however, was not the case. The position of most Liberal Catholic and Modernist Anglicans was that held by Rawlinson, who argued for the maintenance of subscription. His summary contentions were widely shared:

a) Clerical subscription to Prayer Book, Ordinal and Articles is required only in general terms and is susceptible of interpretation in a 'liberal' sense.

b) There is consequently no point at which, *upon the mere ground of the letter of formularies subscribed or recited*, those who are commonly known as the 'liberal' clergy can be attacked in the name of a 'common honesty.'

c) It is not necessarily a dishonest proceeding to recite the creeds in worship with a general intention of being identified with the historic faith of Christendom as a whole, even though an attitude of reserve be maintained in respect to particular clauses in the Creeds.[39]

Two points here continued to dissatisfy High and Low Churchmen, as well as some Liberals. The notion of a general assent remains, in the minds of many clergy and laymen, sorely inadequate. The question raised in the House of Common's debate back in 1865 remains, for many, unanswered: Since the whole is made up of different parts, how can a man of candor feel honest if his general assent does not include assent to the particulars therein? Likewise, is it not dishonest to recite creeds as an expression of unity "with the historic faith of Christendom" when one questions or denies specific doctrines of that faith? The fact is that these very theological formulas were no bond of union, but continued to be the source of the most bitter opposition and division.

On the other hand, what good is subscription to formulas and the recital of creeds if they themselves need to be interpreted and actually admit of many different meanings? Are they not made to say anything and nothing? Does not such a situation repulse a candid man from subscribing? For does it not retard the development of a perfect sincerity? The late Victorians thought so, but fewer and fewer churchmen now felt any urgency in facing such questions.

[1] G. K. A. Bell, *Randall Davidson*, (London, 1938), pp. 397-98.

[2] J. M. Thompson, *Through Facts to Faith* (London, 1912), pp. 208.

[3] H. Hensley Henson, *The Creed in the Pulpit* (London, 1912), p. XV.

[4] *Ibid.*, p. XVI.

[5] *Ibid.*, p. XVII.

[6] Charles Gore, *The Basis of Anglican Fellowship* (London, 1914), p. 12.

[7] *Ibid.*, p. 13.

[8] *Ibid.*, p. 25.

[9] H. M. Gwatkin, *The Bishop of Oxford's Open Letter: An Open Letter in Reply* (London, 1914), p. 5.

[10] *Ibid.*, p. 6.

[11] J. F. Bethune-Baker, *The Miracle of Christianity: A Plea for 'the Critical School' in regard to the use of Creeds* (London, 1914), p. 8.

[12] *Ibid.*, p. 9.

[13] *Ibid.*, p. 11.

[14] *Ibid.*, p. 12.

[15] B. H. Streeter, *Restatement and Reunion*, (London, 1914), p. XIX-XX.

[16] *Ibid.*, p. XX.

[17] *Ibid.*, p. XIX.

[18] *The Basis of Anglican Fellowship*, pp. 19, 20.

[19] Charles Gore, "Symbolism," *The Constructive Quarterly* (March, 1914), p. 61.

[20] This criticism was offered by C. W. Emmet, *Conscience, Creeds and Critics*, (London, 1918), pp. 72-73.

[21] Streeter, op. cit., p. XVI.

[22] *Ibid.*, p. XVII.

[23] William Sanday, *Bishop Gore's Challenge to Criticism*, (London, 1914), p. 12.

[24] *Ibid.*, p. 15.

[25] A. E. Taylor, *The Faith of a Moralist*, II, (London, 1930), 142-43.

[26] Frederic H. Chase, *The Gospels in the Light of Historical Criticism*, (London, 1914), p. VIII.

[27] *Ibid.*, p. IX.

[28] *Ibid.*, p. X.

[29] *Ibid.*, p. XII.

[30] H. Henson, *The Creed and the Pulpit*, pp. IXX-XX.

[31] *Ibid.*, p. XXI.

[32] *The Chronicle of Convocation* (1914), p. 260.

[33] G. K. A. Bell, *Randall Davidson*, p. 683-84.

[34] *Ibid.*, p. 687.

[35] *Ibid.*, p. 688.

[36] *Ibid.*

[37] *Convocation of Canterbury*, 1922 (May 22).

[38] A. E. J. Rawlinson, *Dogma, Fact and Experience*, (London, 1915), p. 207.

[39] *Ibid.*, pp. 204-05.

# Epilogue

A further step in Anglican liberality was taken in 1938, with the publication of the Report of the Commission on *Doctrine in the Church of England*. The Commission had been established by Archbishop Davidson in 1922 at the urgent request of many clergymen. It included many of the most eminent theologians, representing all schools of thought, in the church. The Report upheld general assent to the authoritative formularies as a reasonable expectation from all members of the church. However, general assent, signified by participation in public worship, does not, the Report insisted, imply "detailed assent to every phrase or proposition thus employed."[1] Hence a member of the church "should not be held to be involved in dishonesty merely on the ground that, in spite of some divergence from the tradition of the church, he has assented to formularies or makes use of the church's liturgical language in public worship."[2]

The Report goes on to state a resolution and an hermeneutical rule that represent marked victories for a liberal theology. While requiring that clergy should teach doctrine in accordance with the mind (ambiguous enough) of the church, the Report allowed that an authorized teacher could put forward opinions which diverge from the traditional teaching so long as he is "careful to distinguish between such opinions and the normal teaching which he gives in the church's name."[3]

More significantly, the long-standing distinction between historical and symbolical truth in Scripture and Creed is erased:

> Statements affirming particular facts may be found to have value as pictorial expressions of spiritual truths, even though the supposed facts themselves did not actually happen. . . . It does not appear possible to delimit with finality or precision the extent to which symbolic elements of this . . . kind may enter into the historic tradition of the Christian faith. The possibility cannot be excluded that in this sense also a symbolic character may attach to the truth of articles in the Creeds. It is not therefore of necessity illegitimate to accept and affirm particular clauses of the Creeds while understanding them in this symbolic sense.[4]

As a result of the debates of 1900-1920 over the ethics of belief, the church was, in general, ready to acknowledge that the ethical question was a dangerous red-herring when pursued in isolation from the theological question. But the theological question, it became plain to see, was by its very nature open-ended. Symbolic interpretation reflects the extraordinary latitude that was required by recognition of this fact. There should, of course, be limits. The Report thus attempted, not very happily, to establish a new interpretive fence:

> In some cases the use of traditional phrases is censured as dishonest. This charge could only be sustained if the traditional phrase is being used in a sense wholly different from that originally conveyed by it. . . . The reason for the continued use of such phrases is that *there is a core of identical meaning.* At what point a changed interpretation ethically demands a change in the phrase used is a question to be settled by the moral judgment of the community concerned.[5]

In recent years the English Church, on the whole, has shown slight concern over this moral question. The kind of clear demand put by the liberal Kirsopp Lake is seldom heard. "We would say," Lake wrote in 1918,

> that the figurative method is popular and legitimate, but none the less a mistake. By it anything can be made to mean anything. The true position is that we do *not* accept the Creed *ex animo,* because it represents not our mind but that of a generation . . . mistaken in its view of the interpretation and authority of the Scriptures on which the Creed is based. We refuse either to make the words of the Creed mean what historically they cannot mean, or to accept the position that old answers are sufficient for new questions.[6]

There are those in the English Church today who regard the concerns expressed by Lake as an unhealthy extension of Victorian moral pulse-taking. They argue that demands for radical revision of the Church's formularies or abolition of subscription reflects an extreme present-mindedness. Such a demand, they claim, fails to recognize those profound truths in the tradition which may not be obvious to present experience or the current Zeitgeist. Since some standard of belief is called for, these churchmen argue that the traditional phrases give freer play to the mind than would revised formularies, which will themselves become outmoded in time.

Such a position fails, of course, to take seriously the moral dilemma of the conscientious cleric or churchman. The Report on *Doctrine in the Church of England* leads into that land of "anything can be made to mean anything," so despised by both Bishop Gore and Kirsopp Lake. There is something demoralizing and corrupting in the observance of clerics and laymen subscribing to and rehearsing formularies and phrases which are for them false, problematical, or unmeaning.

There is a further difficulty in the Church's position, as represented in the Report of 1938. Heretical notions now appear impossible in the English Church. Yet it is doubtful that creeds and formularies can mean anything *theologically* without the possibility of heresy. Churchmen now are able to hold that the factual claims and theological doctrines are not essential to Christian belief. R. B. Braithwaite has, for instance, advocated such a position and has received the approbation of some Church of England theologians. According to Braithwaite, the relevant test of Christian belief is whether its stories reinforce the resolution to live a Christian or loving way of life, "but (one) need not believe that the empirical propositions presented by the stories correspond to empirical fact."[7] Braithwaite finds support for his claim in the hermeneutical rule set forth in the 1938 Report on *Doctrine in the Church of England.*

A position such as Braithwaite's does not mean, of course, the demise of a Christian humanism, but it does raise the issue of a Christian *theology*. It was recently commented that while "Christianity . . . embodies insights which were thought by its authors to depend on the truth of certain transcendentalist doctrines. . . . Braithwaite (is) a living proof that Christianity can survive as a medium for the conduct of reflection about men and their lives and their perplexities, even when a belief in its transcendentalist propositions has been abandoned."[8] But if, in fact, the traditional theological assertions are abandoned then subscription to doctrinal articles and the use of traditional phrases in the creeds and liturgies is clearly disingenuous and dishonest because the "core of identical meaning" is dissolved.

This question is not pursued with any thoroughness or enthusiasm by most clergy or churchmen in Britain today. As David Edwards has remarked concerning clerical assent to the Articles, "Like the British weather among intelligent people, it has ceased to be an agreeable subject of conversation. But like Mount Everest 'it is there' "[9] The Report on *Doctrine in the Church of England* was rejected by the houses of Bishops in Convocation as a declaration of the doctrine of the Church. It was received, rather, as "a survey of the currents of thought and belief" and commended for further study. The bishops claimed to recognize the difficulties of scholars and the need for "the fullest freedom of inquiry," but they reminded all churchmen that "the doctrine of the Church of England is now, as it has been in past time, the doctrine set forth in the Creeds, in the Prayer Book, and in the Articles of Religion."[10] The efforts of a minority, led by the Dean of St. Paul's, W. R. Matthews, to revise the Articles, was soundly defeated in 1938, and has gained little support in the years since.[11] The most realistic prospect appears to be for the use of a simpler and more "open" formula of assent.[12]

The Victorians' ethical struggle between a forthright assent to the creeds and standards of the church and the sacred duty of truth seeking and plain speaking is, it appears, a stage of our moral life that is now largely past. It represents what Lionel Trilling has called the sentiment of sincerity, of the "honest soul." In a reminiscence of that older moral sentiment G. M. Trevelyan speaks of the Victorian's debate over the ethics of belief, and of how it was "examined with a clearness and conscientiousness which seems," he regrets, "to have been lost by some of our generation."[13] The price of the struggle was very high, both in personal suffering and corporate strife and division, but the moral corrosion which issues from indifferentism is surely a melancholy sight and full of ominous prospects for religion and society.

With all its limitations exposed and with due modifications made, it would be well if that ethical concern over belief which so exercized the late Victorians would once again be recognized as a moral responsibility. At least Leslie Stephen and his friends believed that no society could long survive the erosion of such a moral ideal—and in this they were surely right.

[1] *Doctrine in the Church of England,* (London, 1938), pp. 38-39.

[2] *Ibid.,* p. 39.

[3] *Ibid.*

[4] *Ibid.,* pp. 37-38.

[5] *Ibid.,* pp. 34-35.

[6] Kirsopp Lake, "The Hereford Appointment," *Hibbert Jounal,* (16), 634.

[7] Renford Bambrough, *Reason, Truth, and God,* (London, 1969), p. 27.

[8] *Ibid.,* p. 152.

[9] David Edwards, "The Thirty-Nine Articles: One Last Heave," *The Modern Churchman,* 10, N. S., (1966-67), 135. A few clergymen such as Canon J. D. Pearce-Higgins and Bishop Hugh Montefiore have, of late, added to their assent a public protest or supplementary declaration—an action which Edwards proposes that others take.

[10] *Chronicle of Convocation,* June, 1938, p. 272.

[11] The Archbishop's Commission on Christian Doctrine, formed in 1967, issued a thoughtful Report on *Subscription and Assent to the Thirty-Nine Articles* (1968). The Commission showed great sensitivity to the moral issue, quoting Principals of Theological Colleges to the effect that "the present requirement . . . tends to bring into disrepute the discipline of the Church of England," and that the state of affairs "only reduced the appearance of honesty in the Church." (30) The Commission offers some, not very convincing, arguments against revision and recommends, as an alternative, a new form of assent, prefaced with a statement indicating that the profession affirms one's "loyalty to this inheritance of faith as your inspiration and direction." (74)

[12] See the recommendation of the Report of the Archbishop's Commission on Christian Doctrine on *Subscription and Assent to the Thirty-nine Articles* (1968).

[13] The loss of concern over the moral issues of religious belief is generally true today as well. An American theologian who has addressed the issues of the ethics of belief is Van A. Harvey. See his *The Historian and the Believer* (New York, 1966), and "Is There An Ethics of Belief," Journal of Religion, 49 (Jan., 1969), 41-58.